RESILIENT

DR. RICHARD K. RAMOS

AUGUST 2020

Charleston, SC
www.PalmettoPublishing.com

Resilient
Copyright © 2021 by Dr. Richard K. Ramos

First Edition

ISBN: 978-1-64990-994-7

DEDICATION

T HIS BOOK IS DEDICATED TO MY MOTHER. IN 1984, SHE divorced my father after 12 years of marriage. Immediately following her divorce, she spiraled downward into a depression. During recovery, I heard my mother speak these words, "I will never get married again for as long as I live." As an impressionable 12-year-old boy, these words resonated loudly and made a lasting impression. I thought marriage must be an unenjoyable experience. If my mother were never to marry again, then I would never even attempt the process. After divorcing my father, I watched my mother suffer in pain and agony to the point of being clinically depressed and under a doctor's care. I did not see her for a six-month period until she was released from a psychiatric ward in a Phoenix hospital. Witnessing that outcome, I wanted nothing to do with marriage.

In October 2009, I met the person I considered to be the love of my life, Mr. Ravin Bridges. I thought the world of him. Together, we pushed through a challenging first year, withstood a move to Connecticut, and made it through his juris doctorate studies. With the passing of Marriage Equality legislation in 2015, we decided to tie the knot. It had taken me 31 years to combat the anti-marriage attitude, but thankfully the arrival had perfect timing. The stage was set, and I had never been more content. We organized a fairytale marriage and planned to live happily ever after. Although the story was cut short after two short years, I still journeyed through the mental roadblock and accepted the idea of marriage. The following story is about resilience, and I dedicate it to my mother in hopes that she will reconsider giving marriage another chance.

I recognize mine did not last long, but I learned so much. Now, I look forward to meeting my next prince charming with a plan to marry and cherish each day together.

We all deserve to be happy and we all have the ability to be resilient. Allow yourself to be loved, Mother. This book is for you.

CONTENTS

FOREWORD...................................... 1

CHAPTER 1 3
The Beginning of the End

CHAPTER 2 16
Sleepless Nights

CHAPTER 3 24
Interventions

CHAPTER 4 33
Choosing Not to Break

CHAPTER 5 39
Awakening

CHAPTER 6 48
Laser Focused

CHAPTER 7 60
Christmas Host

CHAPTER 8 .... **65**
Meeting People

CHAPTER 9 .... **72**
After Marathon Weekend

CHAPTER 10 .... **77**
Divorce Is Final

CHAPTER 11 .... **81**
Time to Defend

CHAPTER 12 .... **88**
Graduation

CHAPTER 13 .... **94**
Germany

CHAPTER 14 .... **100**
Chicago

CHAPTER 15 .... **104**
End of Summer

CHAPTER 16 .... **112**
Cold Hearted

CHAPTER 17 .... **116**
GoFundMe

CHAPTER 18 .... **122**
Relationships

CHAPTER 19 .... **129**
Not Cancer, Again

CHAPTER 20 .... **133**

Hope

CHAPTER 21 .... **138**

More Lies

CHAPTER 22 .... **143**

Pray

CHAPTER 23 .... **148**

Father Figure Farewell

CHAPTER 24 .... **152**

Eulogy

CHAPTER 25 .... **162**

Final Days

CHAPTER 26 .... **166**

Hospice

CHAPTER 27 .... **171**

Aunt Lorraine

CHAPTER 28 .... **176**

Be the Light

CHAPTER 29 .... **188**

Onward

CHAPTER 30 .... **191**

Final Thoughts

FIGURES

Figure 1. Richard Ramos with Uncle Ray Ramos.......90
Figure 2. Richard Ramos with Aunt Lorraine.............175

FOREWORD

Resilient. The act of springing back or rebounding.
—*Webster's Dictionary, 1913*

T HE TITLE OF THIS WORK REVEALS ITS PURPOSE. THE author demonstrates his ability to spring back from the difficulties he has faced, particularly in marriage, relationships, and other personal decisions. He has taken this act of rebounding to another level by helping others, in particular, his family members facing serious medical obstacles and even death. This story of resilience is heart-wrenching yet admirable and always relatable.

As you venture into this work, you may become enamored with the author as you learn about the care he gave his dying aunt and uncle. You likely will find yourself wanting to be part of his life because of his loyalty to family. You may experience gratitude as you learn how he included his brothers in his endeavors to help his dying family members. You might imagine yourself traveling alongside the author as he made various trips to his hometown to check on his aunt and uncle. Through it all, perhaps most illustrative of this family trait of helping others, you'll admire the author's mother as she stands by him as he makes decisions about his aunt's and his uncle's care. You may find yourself drawn to the main characters in this story: his mother, his brothers, his dying aunt, and his dying uncle. You will want to cheer on the author even though he cannot hear you.

The author demonstrates resilience in his ability to continue work on his dissertation even as he meets all the needs of his family, and while maneuvering through a difficult divorce. His story about rebounding is remarkable and will be an inspiration to his readers.

—Margaret M. Carr

CHAPTER 1
THE BEGINNING OF THE END

"OF COURSE, YOU CAN GO TO THE CONCERT ON FRIDAY with your friends. I don't mind. My will for you is your will for you."

I have lived by this motto ever since I first read *Conversations with God: Book One* by Neale Donald Walsch in 2003. I decided to live this way because I do not feel life is about controlling others. Instead, I believe everyone should have the freedom to choose his or her own life's path. As long as you do not hurt anyone else with your choices, you have the will to do what is best for you. I consider myself to be an understanding free spirit. I want to support others as they make good choices and as they strive to be their best selves. Therefore, I choose to live according to the idea that "my will for you is your will for you"—especially with a spouse.

Ravin Bridges, the man I married, asked me if he could go to a concert on Friday, October 27, 2017, at the Crescent Ballroom near Arizona State University (ASU), the downtown campus. He was hanging out with some friends I had never met, and this idea to attend the concert seemed to manifest out of nowhere. According to Ravin, he and his coworker Amir were going to take an Uber to the Crescent Ballroom to meet up with friends to watch a show. Although my intuition told me marriage trouble was looming, I wanted to trust Ravin to do the right thing for both of us. My gut was feeling unsettled and I knew something extraordinary was about to happen. I just did not know my life was about to change drastically overnight.

The week prior, I had noticed Ravin was acting peculiar, doing things I had not noticed before. Perhaps he had displayed similar behavior in the past, but I was extra sensitive to the change this time. During the week, I witnessed Ravin spending an inordinate amount of time in the bathroom feverishly using a vinegar concoction to rid himself of a large, protruding mole that was positioned beneath his pubic hair just above his penis. Suddenly, he became obsessed with its removal and was going to extreme measures to ensure that it was gone.

Throughout the week, I was hypersensitive to everything at home. Intuitively, I felt like something was not quite right, especially in my marriage. Ravin was acting extraordinarily odd. For example, I came home from work one day and noticed both of the chairs at the kitchen table were misplaced. This appeared unusual to me so I asked Ravin if he had company over to the house.

Ravin looked at me and said, "That is a stupid question. No, I didn't have someone over."

Although his response was disrespectful, I didn't respond because I did not want the conversation to escalate, especially if my intuition was inaccurate.

Later in the week, Ravin had sent me a text message while I was working. I read the message, but it made no sense to me.

When I arrived home and was in the bedroom with Ravin, I said, "You sent me a text message today and I couldn't make sense of it. I don't think you intended to send it to me."

Ravin looked at me in disgust and said, "Of course it was meant for you. They were lyrics from a song I played for you last week. Besides, what is the matter with you? Why are you so paranoid this week?"

This time, I responded, "I am your husband. Why are you so mean when I am asking you something so simple? I don't deserve to be spoken to that way."

Internally, I questioned why he was being so defensive. These questions I was asking should have made for easy conversation, especially when being open and honest. With his responses about the chairs being misplaced and the unidentified song lyrics, I started to pay more attention to my intuition. Something was wrong, but at the time, I just didn't know exactly what that feeling was about.

As the week progressed, I was called to the bathroom to help him trim his back and neckline so he could appear clean-cut with a symmetrical line across his hairline. By Wednesday of the week, he called me to the back bedroom so I could help him pick out a "cute" outfit to wear on Friday night to the concert. In addition, Ravin went to a barber to get a haircut to ensure that he looked perfect for the event. By this time, my stomach was unsettled, and I felt as though he was going to something more than a concert. With his mysterious behavior, it appeared to me he was preparing for a date. My only wish was he would be honest with me before boldly making that kind of leap in our marriage.

My intuition was on target. Leaving for the concert, the life I knew transformed in less than 24 hours. I woke alarmed at 3:30 AM in the morning on October 28 to find that Ravin was not sleeping next to me. As usual, I checked my cellphone for messages because it was common practice for Ravin to send text messages when transitioning from one place to another (he did this even when we were dating and lived apart). I received a message at 11:30 PM from Ravin, which read, "I love you more." It was now 3:30 AM, but he had not sent any messages indicating he was too drunk to make it home or that he was staying the night with a friend. Instantaneously, my abdomen was in knots. I felt trouble in my gut.

Still, I wanted to give Ravin the benefit of the doubt. I tried to go back to sleep, but I tossed and turned for an hour while lying in the dark alone. Finally, at 4:30 AM,

I jumped out of bed and headed for the 24-hour gym, Planet Fitness. I was feeling anxious and I needed to destress in some way. In the past, exercise always helped ease my anxiety and preoccupied space in my head.

I wanted to trust Ravin. I did not attempt to call him because I felt it was his responsibility to let me know where he was. I worked out for two hours and returned home; Ravin still had not arrived. Stress mounted once again. This time, I coped with the tension by cleaning the house vigorously. I started with a broom and soon turned to a mop. Time seemed to be ticking slowly as I glanced at the clock just about every minute. At approximately 8:00 AM, I could not take the pressure anymore and I called Ravin. I was concerned about his overall safety and well-being. Perhaps I had watched too many murder mysteries, but I needed to ensure that he was safe and in good health. If something foul had happened to him, I did not want to appear that I did not care about his welfare because there was no record of me looking for him. I needed to know he was alive and well.

Ravin did not answer my call and I got his voicemail greeting. I left a message indicating my concern and asked him to call me out of courtesy to let me know he was okay.

About 15 minutes later, I received a text message that read, "I am okay, Kookoo. I just had a little too much to drink."

Although he messaged me and called me by my pet name, I already knew he was lying about drinking too much, especially in the age of Uber and Lyft.

Shortly after sending the text message, Ravin and I talked on the phone. I was on my way to Lux Café and Ravin called me while I was driving. He said he was walking to Lola Coffee near 3rd Avenue and Roosevelt in downtown Phoenix. I changed directions and told him I would meet him there. He asked me if he could buy my coffee. I agreed and made my way in that direction. We had so much to discuss.

Upon arrival, I parked and walked toward the coffee shop. Ravin was on his way out of Lola and walked toward me. He looked ragged and exhausted. He handed me a coffee and we jumped into my vehicle.

I said, "You look so tired like you didn't sleep. You must be exhausted if you slept on the floor."

Ravin responded, "No, I slept in a bed. I stayed at my friend Armando's house."

That name became my focus, and I wondered who Armando was. It was another name I had never heard before. I became fixated on Armando.

Once driving, I told him we had a lot to discuss. Unfortunately, I had commitments for the day. I had breakfast scheduled with mom at 9:00 AM. In addition, it was homecoming at ASU with a day full of festivities in which I was expected to participate. I was preparing to take Ravin home so he could get some sleep, but he opted to go with me to take my mom to breakfast. This was strange behavior. In the past, Ravin had never wanted to have breakfast with my mom. I did not understand why he had this change of heart: why suddenly would he want to go with me to have break-fast with my mom?

Breakfast was such an uncomfortable experience. I wanted to talk to my mom about the events of the past 12 hours, but Ravin was present and I didn't want an intense conversation. Instead, we all settled on small talk and discomfort. Then, it dawned on me. Ravin wanted to be included at breakfast just so I would not have a conversation with my mom about the night. Just like he had done the entire week, he attempted to manipulate this situation, too.

After breakfast, I took Ravin home and asked him to get some rest. I needed some time to put the day into per-spective and get ready to head out to ASU to participate in the homecoming festivities. I took a drive through the neighborhood and parked at the local elementary school to do some research online. I needed some time to scan the internet for a guy by the name Armando (the person with whom Ravin had stayed the night). I did not have to look too hard.

I opened my Facebook app and searched for Ravin Bridges, Armando, Phoenix, Gay. I hit the search button and, instantaneously, the guy I was looking for appeared on my iPhone screen. I looked at his posted pictures and searched his "likes" to determine whether my husband, Ravin Bridges, had liked any of his photos.

Bingo. I had the right person. Ravin not only "liked" his photos, but he "loved" them.

After confirming I had the right person, I looked for any mutual friends. Low and behold, my cousin Shakira was a mutual friend. Without hesitation, I called Shakira and asked her how she knew Armando Wakefield.

Without much of an explanation, she said, "Don't fuck with him. He sleeps around and gets treated like a bitch by his boyfriend. All those boys I know sleep around."

In response, I said, "Ravin, my husband, stayed the night with Armando last night."

Outraged, Shakira informed me that she was going to reach out to Armando to talk with him about his behavior. I asked her not to contact him because I had all the information I needed. Before hanging up, Shakira assured me she would not contact Armando or say anything yet.

At that point, I ran a few errands before heading to ASU. As a former member of the Leadership Scholarship Program (LSP), I had agreed to attend the tailgate reunion. Afterward, I attended the parade with my brother Gabriel, sister in-law Stacey, and niece Gabriela. We enjoyed the ASU spirit and pride. After watching floats, dancers, and bands, the parade ended around 4:30 PM. Gabriel and I were staying for the football game, so we walked Stacey and Gabriela back to the car so they could make their way home.

As we approached Mill Avenue and University in downtown Tempe, I received a text message from Ravin. It read, "To clearly communicate, I am going to dinner with Armando and I am staying the night. I hope you are okay with that."

Reading that text message, my heart sank to my feet. Inside, I was scrambling and suddenly it became harder to breathe. I did not know who to share the text with at this point. No one knew that our marriage was in this kind of trouble. I questioned whether or not I should make myself vulnerable and share this information. I decided to open up, and I showed my brother the text. I knew this would affect the way I viewed the game, so I thought he should know as we would be watching the ASU game side by side.

As I caught my breath, I responded to Ravin's text message. I let him know I was going to call him in a few minutes. I just needed to find a place where I could be by myself for a few moments to make a call.

As my brother was saying goodbye to his family, I walked across the street to make a phone call. Ravin picked up the phone. Immediately, I informed him I was not okay with his spending the night with someone else. I did not mind his having dinner with another person, but I expected him to be home so we could talk first. Our marriage was in a difficult place, and we needed to sort through the events that had occurred over the past 24 hours.

Ravin's response to my request blew my mind.

He replied aggressively, "I am not coming home!"

Ravin was angry because I would not agree with his desire to spend the night with another man. As his husband, I pleaded with him one more time to come home later so we could talk. Ravin was short with me and made it clear he was not coming home. Therefore, I asked him to make some time so we could talk the following day.

When we hung up the phone, it felt like my life had been sucked out of me. All sorts of alarms were going off in my body. I felt confused and my body was fueled with intense heat. My demeanor about the game changed, and my brother was left to deal with my mood shift.

We headed toward the stadium. As we approached College Avenue, booths and street vendors were set up along the way with free giveaways. I tried hard to distract myself, but I could not take my mind off my personal matters.

While moving through the crowd, I received a phone call from Ravin. I answered the phone because I thought maybe he had a change of heart. Perhaps he was calling to tell me he would meet me back at the house tonight once the game was over. Instead, I picked up the receiver and heard raging anger in his voice.

Ravin shouted, "Richard, why is your cousin Shakira messaging Armando? We have on open relationship. Call your cousin right now and tell her this relationship is open because Armando won't do anything with me now. Besides, she has no business getting involved."

I responded by telling Ravin I was not calling Shakira because I did not agree with his actions. On one hand, our relationship was open, but we were supposed be honest with one another before meeting up with anyone. Dating, on the other hand, was out of the question. My relationship with Ravin was supposed to be his primary relationship; we were married. Spending the night with someone else was not part of our agreement. I always thought coming home to your spouse was the priority.

Obviously, Ravin was not playing by the same rules, and his expectations were never clearly communicated.

Finally, Gabriel and I arrived at the stadium. We found our upper-level seats and prepared to watch the game against the University of Southern California (USC) Trojans. I stepped away to call my cousin Shakira because I needed her to know what was transpiring. I had asked her not to get involved earlier in the day, and I was not sure why she had disregarded my request.

Upon sharing the experience with Shakira, she gave me an earful on the other end of the phone line. She informed me that I should never have opened up my marriage. Shakira did not care that Ravin did not want her reaching out to Armando. She said, "I am not going to let my cousin get fucked over by someone who I considered a friend."

Shakira knew Armando from the past, and therefore, she felt like she had every right to talk with him about his choices. In addition, Shakira had a problem with this ethically because she did not feel Armando should be sleeping with a married man, especially her cousin's spouse. She made it clear that she was not going to stop texting Armando. If Ravin wanted the texting to stop, Shakira wanted him and Armando to call her directly given that they were two grown men. Besides, Armando had her telephone number.

Soon after I hung up with Shakira, Ravin called again. He was even more outraged. He was fuming because Shakira would not stop texting Armando. I informed him I already talked with Shakira and asked her to stop.

Ravin replied, "If you do not get her to stop, I am going to put you on blast on social media."

I reiterated if he wanted Shakira to stop texting, then the two of them should call her and have that discussion.

Ravin became irritated and hollered, "I want a divorce!"

I pulled the phone away from my ear and looked at the receiver with surprise. I had never heard those words from Ravin before. Our marriage was young, and we were just approaching our two-year anniversary.

I responded, "Reserve some time for us to talk tomorrow, I am hanging up the phone now." It was the only thing I could think to say at that point.

I returned to my seat in the grandstands. Again, I turned to my brother for support. My brother described my look as lost and distant. I felt hurt, distracted, and horrified. Supporting the ASU Sun Devil football program was always one of my favorite pastimes, but not even the game could keep my mind occupied. I was facing a mental breakdown filled with emotional turmoil. And my brother was on the receiving end of this downward tailspin.

The game against the USC Trojans was a complete blur. My brother knew I was not healthy mentally. I stared blankly into the night and felt a sense of emptiness as I sat in the middle of a crowded, enthusiastic stadium. My head was pounding and all I could think about was what I did to deserve this outcome. Instantly, I blamed myself and wondered how I could let the relationship get to this point. I thought, "Why didn't you recognize the problems before you allowed this to happen?"

The night was long as the USC Trojans annihilated our Sun Devils. The despair was now doubled. Immediately, I became concerned about traveling home to an empty house. Going home would only be a reminder of the events that had occurred over the past 24 hours. How could I stop this from occurring? What could I do to save this marriage? What did I do to allow this turn of events to happen in my life? So many questions surfaced on the drive home from the game.

I knew one thing for sure: I had to frame this experience differently; otherwise, I was going to be in a world of loneliness when I arrived home. Already, I knew I was in for another sleepless night, but this, too, would pass. I had to prepare for the beginning of the end while still believing, "My will for you is your will for you."

CHAPTER 2
SLEEPLESS NIGHTS

T HE NIGHTS, IN FACT, WERE SLEEPLESS. AFTER ASU
got shellacked by the USC Trojans, I went home. It
was exactly as I thought it would be: quiet, lonely, and
distant. I felt isolated. I took a shower and let the hot
water pour over my body. I wanted so badly for the
steam to melt away the pain. How did we get here so
soon? This question ruled my brain as the minutes
ticked away slowly. Watching the clock was like watching molasses drip from a spigot.

After stepping out of the shower, the challenge of
getting into our bed was even more heartbreaking. As
I pulled the covers over my body, I tossed and turned
throughout the night knowing Ravin was in bed with
someone else. The night was miserably sleepless.

I rose the next morning, hungering for actual sleep. I
called my friend Tracy to meet me for a morning workout. Luckily, she has always been a true friend. Standing
always by my side, she met me at LA Fitness to work out.

She tried desperately to make me laugh and take my mind off the events that had transpired over the weekend. At times, she succeeded, but the pain had a grip on my body like a vice. Sometimes the hold felt barely manageable.

After the workout, I went to Target to buy my nephew Jacob a birthday gift. I was scheduled to attend his birthday party at the Red Robin Gourmet Burgers in Tempe at 3:00 PM. After the party, I made arrangements to meet Ravin at our house at 5:00 PM so that we could speak for the first time since this debacle began. I hoped we could discuss our marriage and expectations moving forward.

I selected a gift card for Jacob's birthday and headed home to take a shower to prepare for his party. Although I was not feeling up to any celebration, I never would miss my nephew's birthday. My body was on fire with the pain, but I pulled myself together enough to make it on time.

From the minute I walked through the door, everything irritated me, ranging from where I sat at the table to the behavior of my family. I did not want to deal with anyone's company. At 4:30 PM, I left the gathering and headed home for a conversation that I knew was about to change everything. I just did not know how extreme the adjustment would be.

Ravin was home when I arrived. Standing at the stove with a spatula in hand, he was preparing meals for the week ahead. As a courtesy, I waited patiently for him to finish cooking. I felt as though I was walking on eggshells waiting for this conversation to happen.

To avoid having an argument instead of a grounded conversation, I knew it was important that I dressed nicely and said the right things. I needed to feel confident in my appearance and wore a mint green V-neck top with khaki bottoms. This was huge as I was about to have one of the most critical conversations in my life.

On the way home, I had rehearsed the conversation in my head so that I could stay focused and on point. I reminded myself to stay calm throughout the discussion and decided it was important to record the dialogue using my iPhone. When Ravin finished cooking and packaging the meals for the refrigerator, I approached the kitchen. I asked him if it was a good time to talk. He agreed.

Taking time on my appearance had worked, and it was the first thing Ravin noticed as I walked toward him.

Ravin complimented me, "You look really cute."

Although I could not reveal how I felt in front of him, I silently chalked one up in the win column.

Making every effort to be a loving spouse, no matter the circumstances, I asked him if he wanted to go for a walk, sit in the backyard, or move to the living room to have this discussion. Ravin chose the living room, and we sat facing each other on the couch. I discreetly started recording our conversation using my smartphone and placed the device facedown on the coffee table. I used this strategy to ensure that I stayed calm and collected no matter what direction our discussion turned.

I asked Ravin if he wanted to start the conversation or if he wanted me to begin. He deferred to me. Because

I was prepared, I told Ravin when I decided to marry him that my decision was definite and that we had one of the most romantic weddings I had ever imagined. In addition, I shared that the marriage was not just a fairy-tale to me.

To my surprise, Ravin responded sarcastically, "Thanks for convoluting everything."

It took everything in my power at that point to stay calm and collected. Thankfully, the recording was rolling and I knew to stay composed.

Based on our past conversations, I should have known Ravin was going to react this way and that the conversation would be challenging. If I wanted this discussion to be productive, I needed to stay poised. When having certain discussions, Ravin always displayed a negative attitude and sarcasm, especially when he had to take responsibility or admit any wrongdoing. At times, it had appeared to me that he had an inferiority complex, so I should have expected this same type of behavior during this conversation.

Ravin cut straight to the chase. He remarked, "There is only one thing we need to talk about and that is an open relationship."

I assumed this was his way of manipulating the conversation. He had been direct about what he needed to discuss, but he had rejected the choice of starting the conversation.

Ravin's reaction took me to a point in the conversation sooner than I anticipated, so I agreed to focus on the open relationship aspect of our marriage. I responded to Ravin by sharing that I did not have a problem with an open relationship. I was fine with the concept. I asked just two things to move forward. First, I expressed how important it was for spouses to come home at night and sleep next to each other. Second, I communicated I felt it was vital to our marriage to refrain from starting additional relationships on top of ours. To me, this would make our marriage too challenging, and we would lose focus on which relationship was the primary relationship.

To my surprise, Ravin snapped back, "I can't do that, I am polyamorous, and I want a divorce."

My heart dropped to my feet again. This was the second time Ravin had raised the issue of divorce in less than 24 hours. I had not rehearsed this part of the conversation and was baffled.

I responded, "Ravin, if that is what you want, you're going to have to move out."

Now, Ravin was surprised. He was shocked and asked me when I wanted him out of the house.

I responded, "Today is Sunday and I would like you out by Friday."

Ravin explained he was unsure whether he could find a place to live in such short notice.

I had to protect myself. My world was being rocked, and I did not expect our conversation to spiral downward so quickly. My body was filled with fear, and I could not see the future clearly any longer. Everything shifted and my emotions suddenly were scattered into a million pieces.

After removing myself from this discussion, I moved to the dining table and sat for a few moments letting my tears flow. I needed to release the emotions I had been feeling over the course of the whole weekend. The hurt was beyond measure and letting tears roll down my face was a form of relief. The pain pierced my heart, but I had the answers I needed. I knew deep down the marriage was over.

For eight years, I had watched Ravin Bridges treat others disrespectfully, manipulate situations for personal gain, and repeatedly strike with vindication to even a score. Now, I felt like I was on the receiving end of his game. For years, as I watched his behavior in horror, I promised myself I would leave the relationship if he ever turned the tables on me. Suddenly, the table had turned, and I had to honor my self-promise and leave the relationship without looking back. The person I loved the most in the world had let me down.

To describe my emotions as anger was far from what I felt. I was more disappointed in myself for being so vulnerable. With Ravin Bridges, I had invested so much time and energy. I also had let down my guard. I shared every facet of who I was in this marriage. This behavior contradicted my upbringing, as I had been groomed by both sides of my family to never get married.

According to my family members, marriage was problematic. Not even my grandparents were married. My parents, in contrast, had married but even that ended in divorce. From my perspective as a young child, marriage just brought on all sorts of issues. The relationships that were modeled before me were completely unhealthy. Agreeing to marry Ravin was totally against all the advice I had received throughout my life. I went against the will of my family and took a chance. The person I considered to be my true love betrayed me; and, for the first time in a while, I felt a great sense of fear.

Immediately, I called one of my teachers, Tony Knowles, and asked him if I could come over to his apartment. At the time, I was a principal of an elementary school, and Tony was my confidante at work. He had become my friend over a four-year period. Thankfully, he was home and told me he would be waiting for me.

I drove to his house and he was waiting for me outside his apartment gates. Tony was the most empathetic person in this situation. I shared the weekend events, including the fact that I would be getting a divorce. Already, he was aware we were having some problems because I had talked to him about some of the conversations I had been having with Ravin over the summer. Although he knew of our problems, he did not realize this was going to lead to divorce.

Tony was accommodating and asked what I needed from him at that moment. In addition, he offered me a place to stay at his apartment and more time to discuss the events surrounding the weekend. I assured him I would be fine and lending his ear was enough for now. I left Tony's apartment and headed home to start picking up the pieces from a life that had just been dismantled.

I needed to prepare for a conference that was happening the very next day at the Black Canyon Conference Center in North Phoenix. I was devastated and tired of the sleepless nights.

CHAPTER 3
INTERVENTIONS

R AVIN AND I SLEPT IN THE SAME BED THAT SUNDAY
night. Although we slept side-by-side, I had never
felt more distant. I knew we were in the middle of a crisis, and my body hurt all over. Emotions were high, and
I felt like I was in the midst of losing a battle. I had a
difficult time understanding why he wanted to be there
and under the same sheets, other than for comfort.
Although I felt like I was losing him, a part of me did not
want him to leave.

On Monday morning, I woke up and made breakfast
for the both us, as usual. I prepared his food and put it
into a container to refrigerate until he woke up later. In
addition, I wrote Ravin a routine love note and stuck it
to the mirror in the bathroom before I left.

The moment I left the driveway, intense anxiety surfaced as soon I closed the car door. I was on my way
to a conference in North Phoenix at the Black Canyon
Conference Center when I saw a Starbucks nearby at

Glendale and the Black Canyon Freeway. I had a book on leadership with me so I decided to pull over, sip on a cup of coffee, and read for a while. I thought it would ease my mind from the personal problems at home. Unfortunately, that did not work, and so I packed up my things and got back on the road to the conference.

Outside the building, I waited for my boss to arrive at the conference. I had been thinking about interventions I needed to put in place so I did not spiral downward and into a deep depression. I had not felt this empty in a really long time. I needed to set up some supports to deal with what I considered to be a traumatic experience. Some interventions that worked for me in the past had been daily exercise, regular appointments with a psychotherapist, taking a slight dosage of an antidepressant, and ensuring that I stayed connected with a social network. I was in the middle of writing a dissertation as a doctoral student, and I was five months away from defending my research.

In the parking lot, I waited for my boss to arrive so I could share my experience with her before taking the first step toward putting these interventions in place. I needed to see my family medical practitioner to request an antidepressant to make it through this ordeal in the midst of completing my research. At the time, I was collecting data and writing the next two chapters of my dissertation. I could not let my world crumble after coming this far in my doctoral studies.

I knew my boss would understand so I waited outside the conference. In addition, she needed to know some background information in the case this ordeal affected my abilities at work as the principal of an elementary school.

While I awaited my boss' arrival, I called my doctor's office to explain I needed to see my doctor as soon as possible—it was urgent. Luckily, an appointment was available around lunchtime, so I confirmed the time.

For me, it was imperative I see my doctor to ask for an antidepressant. I needed balance; I could not allow myself to slip into a depression. I had so much work to do on my dissertation. I had felt this type of pain only one other time in my life, and I did not want to revisit those feelings of loss, fear, and disparity. It took me awhile to agree to take an antidepressant back then; but when I did, it had helped me balance my emotions, and I was able to get some much needed rest at night.

I knew this would all be temporary and I was racing against time. I needed to move past this situation and get back to work on my dissertation. I did not have time to fall behind. I was just five months away from completing my research, defending my work, and graduating from ASU.

My boss arrived, and I shared my situation. She was in complete disbelief. I told her about my doctor's appointment at noon, and she agreed it was a good idea for me to go to my doctor for advice and get the balance I needed. Throughout the morning portion of the conference, I was beyond miserable. I was anxious and full of grief. I felt as though I was unraveling in layers in front of an audience. The only thing on my mind was seeing my doctor to get a dosage of medication to help me sleep. I did not want to feel this type of pain; I hurt all over my body. My heart pounded with intensity, and my head felt full of pressure.

In addition to the doctor, I reached out to a former elementary school counselor through email and requested a list of psychotherapists she might know. I wanted to make an appointment to talk with a mental health professional. Megan, my former employee, sent me a list of five resources. I started to recognize at this time of need that my friends were showing up, and I was grateful. I chose two therapists from the list and called both without getting answers so I left voice messages. I knew how busy therapists happen to be in the 21st century; therefore, by calling two, I would receive a call back from at least one of them. Thankfully, one of them called me back within 24 hours and I had an appointment scheduled for the next week. I felt as though I was putting all the right resources in place.

It had not even been 24 hours since my life had changed drastically. I had an understanding boss, an appointment with a doctor to get an antidepressant, and a scheduled meeting with a psychotherapist. Because of the rapid time in which everything occurred, I was fortunate to be able to put the necessary resources in place to improve my mental and emotional health.

At noon, I went to the doctor, and after learning about my situation, he immediately prescribed an anti-depressant medication. He was so empathetic about my personal situation and there were no questions asked. The doctor had my medical history; therefore, he knew about the medication I had been taking in 2003, which was the last time I was feeling this way. He prescribed me the same drug and dosage. In addition, he asked me to stay in contact with him to ensure that I was okay and to communicate a request for change in dosage, if necessary. I absolutely agreed to stay in contact.

It appeared like I was laying a foundation for recovery and I felt so grateful. After my appointment, I went back to the conference and prepared to pick up my medication immediately following the conference.

Next, it was critical to set up an appointment with my dissertation chair, Dr. Manuel Kim. At the orientation of my doctoral program, school officials addressed the candidates by acknowledging the time commitment it would take to complete this particular leadership and innovation doctoral program. During the opening message, professors shared with candidates that they should not plan any life-altering events during the tenure of the program. It was recommended not to have children, get married, or go through a divorce. The coursework was so demanding that these life-changing events had the potential to derail progress. Therefore, telling Dr. Kim I was about to get a divorce was a conversation I was dreading, but he needed to know in case I was unable to carry on with my research.

As I was in the middle of implementing my intervention with third- and fourth-grade teachers at Star View

STEM Academy, I had one more professional development session to implement. In addition, I needed to collect data in the form of classroom observations, collect teacher journal entries, conduct participant interviews with both teachers and students, and arrange a final focus group interview with teachers. My project required an enormous amount of work and this juncture was critical.

After collecting data, I had to analyze the information to write the chapter 4 that included the data collection results, as well as the chapter 5 that summarized the entire research venture. The completion of this action research project was dependent on the work I was doing at that very moment.

After Ravin's disclosure, I was very numb. At times, I felt stuck and could not move forward. Therefore, I contacted Dr. Kim for a meeting out of great need. We met near ASU out of convenience. As soon as we sat down, I realized that he thought our discussion was going to be about the progress I was making on my research. He asked, "What kind of progress are you making?" I shared with him that I needed to talk to him about a personal matter. When I disclosed I was getting a divorce, to my surprise, he was extremely empathetic. Although he did repeat that I was not supposed to make any life-altering decisions like this over the course of the doctoral program. I assured him that it was not my decision, but the choice of my spouse.

At that point, he took immediate control of the situation. He provided some of the most profound advice—it was impressive. With his experience, he told me to take some time to grieve the loss. He asked me to stop writing and take two weeks off from the project. I was astonished because I did not know him to have this capacity as he was so demanding with high expectations. During class and throughout the program, Dr. Kim was extremely driven, but when talking to him, I instantly saw him in a different light—he was showing compassion. Dr. Kim told me that I could take only two weeks to grieve; otherwise, it would be too hard to catch up, and I would not be able to finish the dissertation. I took his advice to heart and implemented this plan at once.

After this conversation, I brought him up to speed on where I was with my project. He was content with my progress and told me to reach out to him if I needed any assistance. I felt much more comfortable after having this meeting, I knew I was in the right place with the right mentor. The conversation also signified that he could be understanding depending on the situation. This was different than the way I had perceived him in the past.

After that meeting, I was relieved and on my way to recovery. I had another resource in my corner. I left this meeting feeling supported and felt like I could still reach success if I followed his suggestions, allowing for a two-week grieving process and returning to my research immediately afterward.

To further distract myself, I contacted a former student, Joshua Mendez. I had been following him on

Instagram and recognized he landed in the business of fitness training. I admired this young man as a student and learned a lot from his Instagram posts about physical activity. Therefore, I reached out to Joshua for private lessons. I also thought it would be a great intervention to ensure good health during this challenging time. Having messaged him on social media, I was fortunate again: Joshua had a 5:40 AM workout class available and I was able to start the following week. I agreed to work out on Mondays and Wednesdays. In addition, I scored again when he informed me I would get his family discount because I was his former teacher. Moving forward, I paid Joshua $240 a month to get in the best shape possible to maintain mental sanity. I agreed to take the risk and trained with my newest trainer for 40 minutes twice a week.

After speaking with Joshua, I was feeling really good inside because various resources appeared to be surfacing in my life. First and foremost, my supervisor was really sympathetic and offered me any support I needed. Second, my dissertation chair was helpful and offered sound advice to ensure that I had the time to grieve yet succeed by setting a timeline. Third, I secured the antidepressant medication to help me chemically balance my emotions, knowing this was just a temporary solution. Fourth, I made contact to discuss my situation with a psychotherapist as an outlet for additional professional support with life and logic. Fifth, I was now scheduled to receive physical fitness training with a former student to ensure that my mind, body, and spirit were aligned. Finally, my friends and family were there to support me as well.

Everyone seemed to come to my rescue. My friends were not going to allow me to fail. Already, the road to recovery appeared to be inevitable. I could see light at the end of this dark hour. I went to bed that Monday night stabilized knowing these interventions were in place.

CHAPTER 4
CHOOSING NOT TO BREAK

AFTER A LONG DAY AT WORK, I WAS DRIVING HOME AND reflecting on the divorce. Being honest with myself, I was having second thoughts about this choice. It was Halloween, so I decided to stop by the grocery store to buy candy in case trick-or-treaters knocked at the door. While shopping, I mustered up the courage to have one more conversation with Ravin about the divorce topic. I arrived at home, put the candy on the counter, and found Ravin in the house. Walking toward him, I asked if we could talk because I was questioning our decision. I began by asking him to be patient because I wasn't sure we were making the right decision. Pleading my case, I shared that I had a lot on my plate and perhaps we should take it slow. I asked him to allow me to finish writing my dissertation and preparing the defense, which would take about five months. After this period, if we still felt the same way in a few months, then we could proceed.

Ravin turned to me in disbelief and said, "I am not going to put my feelings aside because timing is bad."

At that moment, I recognized divorce was inevitable. I was devasted. His response was cold and selfish. This was someone I spent eight years of my life beside, yet I never felt more isolated. I had no choice but to keep moving forward.

Taking my professor's advice, I stopped writing cold turkey. I needed time to process this experience and allow myself to just grieve. This permitted me to be okay in the moment. The medications appeared to be working, but part of me was still numb from everything happening around me. This was all right, too, because I knew there would be an end to the medication and this feeling of unknowing. I felt everything changing, and I only had a two-week window to make a complete transformation.

I started fast and furiously by rearranging furniture throughout the house. Ravin had taken only a few things when he moved, and I wanted to rid myself of his existence. Anything that was his had to be packed away in boxes and stored in the shed. I boxed all of his items and put them in the standalone shed in the backyard. It felt good to clear my mind from the daily reminders that had been lying around the house. Feeling like everything was out of sight, I was able to start moving past this whole ordeal. The only thing I kept inside the house was his desk and chair, which I moved to the spare bedroom.

The third bedroom had been used as storage when we lived together and a lot of boxes had piled up in this particular space since our wedding. Rummaging through those boxes, I put anything I would not use immediately in the shed. This cleared out the room and made space for Ravin's desk and chair.

Within the week, I hired my brother to paint three rooms in the house. I paid him $100 per room to paint each an earth-tone shade. To further distance myself from the way things used to be, my brother painted the kitchen, bathroom, and the bedroom that I once shared with Ravin. The kitchen was painted a color similar to the original, olive green, but flat paint was used this time. The bathroom was painted with an eggshell white, which was a drastic change from the dark gray we had from before. Finally, my bedroom was painted a flat silver shade. Simultaneously, I hired someone to paint the exterior of the house. Money was not an issue at this point. I just needed to make big changes. I had been saving money for a remodel and had about $7,000 in a savings account. I had been saving money because Ravin and I had talked about renovating the bathroom before the drastic decision he made to leave the relationship. Therefore, I used this money to paint the exterior of the house, too. This was all accomplished within a two-week period during the grieving process.

After all was said and done, I paid about $2,400 to paint the home exterior a light gray with a dark gray trim and a yellow door. The color of the door was the most important part for me. I love contemporary styles and this was the epitome of modern. In addition to painting the interior and exterior, I shopped and bought all new furnishings for the living room. I purchased a new rug, couch, desk, and standing mirror. They were great additions for the transformation I needed. All of the existing furniture, I moved to the den and made it look like a mini-theater. Again, this was a dramatic shift to start my new life. I bought a bed for $80 at a yard sale that I happened to stumble upon while I was leaving World Market. The daybed was a perfect addition for the guest bedroom, especially now that all of the boxes were being stored in the shed out back. Everything seemed to fortunately be falling into place, especially as I only had two weeks to get this completed. I was so grateful I had that savings account to make these significant changes.

Near the end of that two weeks, I received a text message from Ravin letting me know he was ready to pick up the rest of his belongings from the house. I agreed to a time for him to come and told him he had a four-hour window to pick up the items. I would leave the house during that period of time and return some time later. In case he needed more time, he agreed to let me know by text. I gave him the new code to the security system at the house. He immediately questioned why I had the code changed to the security system. I am positive he was thinking I changed the code to keep him away. That was not the case at all. I had changed the code because many workers had been in and out of the house painting and delivering furniture. While they worked on the house, I gave them the original code for convenience. After their work was completed, I changed the code because I did not want them to have access to the house any longer. Again, I assured Ravin that it was not because I did not want him in the house; instead, it was because of the service personnel.

The day arrived for Ravin to pick up his items. I left the home knowing full well he would be there for four hours. I busied myself during that time. At some point, I got a text message from Ravin letting me know the house looked so different. He informed me he loved the furniture, the exterior paint, and the changes made throughout. I felt good about getting this text message. It was great reinforcement that I was making progress under these unusual circumstances. Instead of dwelling on the negative experience, I changed my focus by putting my entire being into making positive change. I am grateful I had the money in savings to make those enhancements. Although this money was supposed to be used for a bathroom renovation, I decided to upgrade the home in a different way, and it did not cost nearly as much. In addition, the furniture was available at bargain prices and worked perfectly.

I truly believe the best way to show someone you are not broken is to rise above the challenges. By making major improvements to your life, those who are a part of your life are forced to notice the transformation is critical to success. This was definitely a start of a new life and a new way of being because what happens next signaled another major adjustment. Although life was a challenge for the moment, I made a conscientious choice not to break.

CHAPTER 5
AWAKENING

Every year, Ravin and I hosted Thanksgiving dinner. Before he left the relationship, we had planned to have people over for Thanksgiving 2017 as well. We even purchased a new oven for our home to cook the turkey for the feast. When our relationship came to a drastic end, for a split second, I considered canceling the celebration. Then, I thought about the people we invited and figured they deserved a place to gather. This fiasco happened so close to holidays and to change plans on short notice would have been unfair to the guests who already accepted the invitation. Therefore, I proceeded as planned and prepared to host our annual Thanksgiving celebration without Ravin. The guest list stayed intact, which included his best friend Bill, mother Susan, and nephew Thomas.

Like always, I wrote a Thanksgiving prayer before digging into dinner. I did not want this experience to be any different. As usual, I recognized every person at the table and shared their significance in our lives. Because of my emotional state, I worked desperately to stick to my script.

Following is the prayer I read before dinner that night:

> Dear Creator, thank you for blessing us with this beautiful meal. Many hands of love went into the preparation of this food. I am grateful for the many contributions.

> If you made it through the front door of this house, we are more than friends, you are my family. When you are family, you are my lifeline. For each and every one of you, I am grateful.

> I am a person of stories, therefore, please bear with me. About a month ago, my life suddenly changed without notice. Up to that point, I was living in the clouds above, thinking life was just perfect. I was happy with my husband, home life, and career. Suddenly, life upended in an instant with one simple text message. As I think about the last six months honestly, perhaps it was more than a text message. My husband had been telling me all along that he was not happy with simple gestures like "I miss San Francisco," "We don't have any friends," and "We never go out." Because life was busy as I worked on my doctorate, I urged him to find that happiness, and if there was

something I could do to help, to let me know. That leads us to where we are today. I love my husband dearly and unconditionally. I want him to be happy and I wish him many years of success. Prince [Ravin's nickname], wherever you are, I love you more!

During this whole ordeal, I kept my eyes wide open. I had a wonderful support team. The first weekend alone, I called my friend Andy Sword to go to breakfast. I gave him my wedding ring and told him to put it in a safe place. For me, it was important it was out of reach because there were many times I felt like flinging it halfway around the world. Andy gladly took the ring, and I know it is secure.

I was open to the many doors that opened as well. The second weekend, I called Sandra Gomez and Tracy Root to meet up for group therapy. Sandra was coming from the Northwest, Tracy from the North, and me from the East Valley. So, we met in the middle at First Watch on Dunlap and the I-17. I arrived first and ran into Dr. Chad Gestson, the superintendent of Phoenix Union High School District. In the past, he was the principal of Camelback High School when I was principal at Madison Park Middle School. Our kids fed into his high school after eighth grade.

At the restaurant, we greeted each other and he asked me what I was doing professionally at the moment. When I told him I was still a principal and getting my doctorate at ASU, he requested a business card and asked me if I was interested in being a principal at a high school. When I agreed, he said he would reach out to me on Monday. He did just that, and I am going to a Phoenix Union workshop on public speaking Tuesday, and on December 12 I have a meeting with the assistant superintendent to discuss shadowing a Phoenix Union principal. For this opportunity, I am grateful.

Soon, I connected with my former student Joshua Mendez. In two weeks, this man helped me transform my body. It has been an intense 40-minute workout although we do not do anything extraordinary. Finally, I now have the six-pack abs I have always wanted. I am so proud of my former student Joshua for making me sweat and nearly cry in the gym. For this, I am grateful.

My beautiful home! I am so glad I had this time to be creative. All the anger and frustrations were channeled toward being creative to update my home. I had a vision for this home since moving back from Connecticut in

2013. I could never get to the renovation due to the late nights of studying and the endless hours of dissertation writing. With the recent change of events, I became persistent in home improvement. Thanks to my brother Anthony, whom I could never repaid for all the coats of fresh paint on the interior walls. In addition, I hired an exterior painter to accomplish the contemporary coating. Additionally, I went on a shopping spree, buying all new furniture and accessories to support the change. The transformation is quite amazing and for that, I am forever grateful.

As for my dissertation, I abandoned that project for about two weeks as I worked on my mental health and sanity. I informed the chair of my committee that my marriage was in trouble and we had an emergency meeting. He told me this was not a good time for this to happen. So together we put a plan in place in the following order: work on your marriage, allow healing time, and get back to your dissertation. I have been back at my dissertation for the last week, and I believe I can catch up. I am grateful for my chair and his wisdom.

Today, I received another blessing. My friend Crystal responded to a post on Facebook. In the comments section, Crystal shared she was so glad Ravin and I found each other. I felt guilty because she did not know the current state of our marriage. So I called her and updated her on the change. We cried together and she informed me that she had been thinking about me all week. Crystal had been working on a Kids Beat television series and was involved in doing an episode on kids with parents who were in prison. They had trouble finding a Caucasian kid who fit this description in New York City. When they did, he was older at the age of 13 years than the rest of the kids. When the kid, Todd, was interviewed by one of the Muppets, he told a story about his dad being incarcerated.

When the Muppet asked, "How do you deal with your situation?" the kid replied, "I have this strategy that I turn every negative into a positive. So I wrote a book and I am helping other kids be positive."

Crystal said that she thought of me when she heard Todd because I try like hell to turn every negative into a positive, and now I am living this experience in this dark hour. For this exchange, I am grateful for friends like Crystal.

In addition, today, out of nowhere, I had a former student reach out to me because he was confused about my post on Facebook. When I told him the state of current affairs, he said, "Mr. Ramos I have had a crush on you since middle school. Do you mind if I take a flight out to come see you this weekend?"

I was flattered, agreed to his visit, and I would pick him up at 10:45 that night. He's only 23 years of age, but I agreed to his visit as a form of distraction.

The following bulleted lines are to those I am so grateful for:

- Mom, thank you for giving your unconditional love.
- Anthony, I appreciate you being the handyman. I could never repay you for your efforts.
- Gabriel, I am so grateful for your support, forks up.
- Stacey, thank you for being my stability and balance.
- Gabby, thank you for teaching me to keep it simple.
- Jake, welcome home. I am so glad you are back. We missed you.
- Alynna, thank you for always being so enthusiastic. I feel your energy.
- Susan, I appreciate your listening to me ramble.
- Aunt Sally, thank you for always being so loyal.

- Michael, you are my rock, thank you for being strong.
- Deedra, I am so grateful to have you in my life.
- Justin, you are full of spirit and energy. Use it to your advantage.
- Landon, although you are young, I can already see you are a risk taker.
- Bill, you are like my foundation at the moment, thank you.
- Rosie, thank you for always allowing me to be open and honest.
- Rigo, you are so dedicated and I am grateful for you.
- Amanda, thank you for sharing your wisdom, I appreciate you.
- Sara, you are my soulmate, my friend. Thank you.

For all of you, I am thankful! If you made it through the front door of this house, we are more than friends, you are my family. If you are my family, you are my lifeline. For each and every one of you, I am grateful.

I stuck with tradition and shared the significance of every guest at the table. Not an eye was dry before dinner that evening. We ate and valued each other's company. Although it was a different experience with Ravin's absence, I knew I was surrounded by amazing people. Already, I felt the tide shifting. The phone conversation I had with my friend Crystal earlier in the day was pivotal. When she shared the story about Todd, the 13-year-old boy, it reminded me of who I was. All my life, I have struggled. But I always try to find the positive in every situation. Just like Todd, I found something good in every experience, including this separation from my spouse. I just needed to wait patiently. I am so glad I had not canceled Thanksgiving 2017 for I was already able to see I was awakening.

CHAPTER 6
LASER FOCUSED

GETTING BACK TO WRITING MY DISSERTATION WAS essential if I wanted to graduate on time. I had to shift my focus immediately away from loss and separation and again immerse myself in research. In the months ahead, I had to train teachers on differentiated instructional strategies with an emphasis on learners who were accelerated or deemed gifted. In addition, I had to collect the last of the data through observations, journal entries, individual interviews, and a final focus group interview. After collecting the data, I had to sort and analyze the material to create the narrative for the "Data Analysis Results" of my dissertation. The final chapter would be due soon after, which was the "Summary of the Research Project." The next few months were going to be intensely busy. Although it felt strange to make such a drastic shift personally, I did not have time to linger and my choices were limited if I wanted to finish on track.

While completing my dissertation, I had a full-time job as an elementary school principal. Spending approximately 60 hours a week at work was also demanding. I was expected to perform my daily responsibilities at a high level. In this role, stakeholders, such as students, teachers, and parents are quite demanding. Finding balance was a task in itself in addition to completing research.

Fulfilling part of my duties as a principal, I attended a workshop in downtown Phoenix on December 8, 2017. I was at the office of Maricopa County Educational Service Agency (MCESA) near downtown Phoenix when I received a text message in the middle of my training. I looked down at my phone and could see the text message number was from Ravin. I had already erased his number from my electronic phone book and unlisted him from my favorites on my cellphone. Still, I recognized his number and it took everything in my power not to read his text. I could not read it just then because I did not want it to negatively affect the way I felt about the conference. Also, I was on solid ground at work and laser focused on writing my dissertation; therefore, I could not afford to be distracted at this point.

At lunchtime, I read the text message. I had not exchanged text messages with Ravin for about three weeks, since he had been at the house to collect his belongings, and getting this text message came from left field. I was completely surprised by this method of communication, especially with the content of the text. Reading the message, Ravin opened by telling me he hoped I was well. Messages I received from him that started this way always appeared to be so superficial. I always felt as though he was not sincere because if he genuinely cared about my well-being, he would not have left the relationship this way. I was insanely busy, working, and going to school to make our lives better and he chose to upend our eight-year relationship abruptly. Together, we ventured to Connecticut for two years. In addition, I had supported him for three years of law school at Berkeley, which included co-signing on his apartment when he had no one else with a credit score high enough to help him. Spending three years apart while he attended law school was tough, but we made it through that challenge. Even though I was busy in the doctoral program, which was five months away from completion, we should have been able to make it over this hurdle, too.

When I started my doctoral program, I asked for Ravin's permission as he was almost done with law school. I wanted his consent because it was going to be labor intensive and would affect our relationship. He not only agreed, but we also made other decisions that were going to have an impact on our life together. Money was an issue, so we agreed I would support our family once he graduated by paying the mortgage and all utilities so that he could pay back his student loans, which had a balance of close to $200,000. This was to occur over five years and then we would reverse responsibilities. After five years, he was going to take on financial responsibility and I would have the chance to pay back my student loans. So, for two years,

Ravin had lived free of mortgage payments and paid large payments to his student loans. Suddenly, he selfishly left the relationship and he was already seeing someone else secretly. Ravin never lived up to the deal or paid me for supporting him while we had lived together. I was never going to get the benefit of paying back my student loans without other financial obligations. So well-wishes were hollow words, and none of his decision-making declarations made sense to me.

Reading the remainder of the text message, Ravin informed me he had filed for divorce. My eyes widened because I felt as though this was too soon. We needed to make that decision together. For him to take this leap was so self-centered. In his text message, Ravin also shared he wanted to serve me rather than having a stranger show up with paperwork. It was lunchtime on a Friday afternoon, and I was astonished to say the least. I felt as though life-altering moments like this one should be discussed thoroughly to determine the best timing for both parties. Life was already intense for me as I was in the middle of deadlines for research and I could not afford to be under any new stresses. I needed a little more time to accept all the changes occurring in my life; this fast timing was definitely unexpected. We had been separated for only one month and already I was faced with this dilemma of signing divorce paperwork.

Letting his text message marinate, I did not respond to Ravin immediately. I thought about the idea for a while during the remainder of the conference. A co-worker,

Mr. Adams, was attending this training with me, and I happened to run into him during a restroom break. He could tell something was bothering me and asked if I needed anything. I quickly shared my dilemma and his feedback was simple and direct.

Immediately, Mr. Adams said, "It is his loss and if he does not want to be with you; go and sign the paperwork to get it over with." Now that was confirmation and just about all I needed. I was not only leaning toward signing on the dotted line, I was close to leaving the conference to get it done as soon as possible. I needed to talk to just one more person before moving in that direction.

During the same break, I called my mother to tell her Ravin had filed for divorce. Discussing this with my mom was probably not the best thing to do as she never had liked Ravin for me. Providing her with this information only added fuel to the fire. Trying not to demonstrate any distaste for Ravin, my mother advised me to go sign the paperwork at once.

She said, "Get it over with because he obviously doesn't want to be married."

My mother advised me to sign the paperwork imme-diately. Now, I was positive I was going to proceed with a signature.

At the end of the MCESA training, I text messaged Ravin. In short, I informed him I would sign the paper-work and I was on my way at once. In response to my message, Ravin was surprised I was coming so soon. It was not what he expected.

Mr. Adams and my mother were right. I needed to get this done and over with and to get on with my life. I could not think about the pain and hurt any longer. Instead, I had to focus on being a principal, completing research, defending a dissertation, and graduating from ASU with a doctorate. I was driven to move to the finish line and Ravin suddenly became a distraction. If he could not respectfully give me the time to complete my coursework, then I did not need him in my life. As hard as it was to accept this idea at the time, he was not the right person for me.

Ravin must have perceived I wanted the divorce, too, because I was on my way to sign the papers the same day he sent his text message. Wanting the divorce was not the case, but I just did not have the fight in me. I had to maintain a focus on job, mental wellness, and research completion. While on my way to the Phoenix downtown area, I text messaged Ravin so we could meet at Wells Fargo near his building. Leaving MCESA, I was only a few miles away. I wanted to meet at Wells Fargo because I was positive that was where he may have met his new boyfriend Armando Wakefield. After some research, I knew Armando was a home loan officer located at the branch downtown conveniently next to Ravin's office. Adamantly against the idea, Ravin did not want to meet at Wells Fargo because according to him, a more private setting would suffice. To me, nothing was private about this situation. Let it be known, we were divorcing, and I was not taking any ownership in this decision. This is not the direction I would have taken, but I felt like it was out of my control. Instead of Wells Fargo, Ravin recommended a Starbucks at a hotel a couple streets away from his office building. I wanted this meeting over with as soon as possible, so I agreed to meet there.

Arriving at Starbucks first, I found the restroom in the building to freshen up. Soon after, I found my way to the counter, ordered a tea, and made my way to a table. Waiting for Ravin to arrive, he appeared with a folder in his hand. As he approached the table, Ravin noticed I had a pen prepared to sign away.

Immediately, he said, "You aren't going to need that pen because I am just going to review the paperwork and you actually need a notary as a witness when signing these documents."

To his surprise, I informed Ravin I was headed to Wells Fargo across the way to sign the paperwork with a notary after our meeting. Then, I would have the documents back to him at his office within minutes. Ravin was astonished with my declaration: one, because I surprised him by meeting him on the same day of his text; and, two, I was driven to sign the divorce papers and return them so rapidly. His actions showed he did not want to be married.

It did not take long for the conversation to change. Ravin commented on my physique, which had changed drastically since he left the month before. He commented on the weight loss and informed me that I looked "good." In addition, he admired my new haircut and was extremely inquisitive. Ravin wanted to know how I was doing. I assured him I was doing well. I shared things were going well as a principal, my research was coming together, and I was analyzing data to write my next chapter. I returned the question and asked how things were going for him.

To my surprise, Ravin responded, "I will get there."

I was sad for Ravin because he chose his current situation. He left a solid relationship with a man who loved him to his core and unconditionally. I would have done anything in the world for him, including allowing him to sleep with other men. All he needed to do was communicate with me and come home at night. Instead, he chose a land of uncertainty. Knowing Ravin, he was thinking too much, and I am sure he was confused.

For context, I was in that same place 12 years earlier, and it had led me to a land of depression and desperation. At that time, I had ended a relationship with a boyfriend of six years. Within weeks, I started seeing someone else, which had lasted only a few months. The new person was unstable and our relationship was unhealthy. In addition, I was not over my ex-boyfriend of six years before starting something new. So when the short-term relationship was over, I was recovering from both endings and was marred by separation. It was intense, and I plummeted into sadness. Therefore, I could relate to Ravin. Our relationship lasted eight years, and only time heals an ending like ours.

As our conversation ended at Starbucks, I followed through on what I said and ventured over to Wells Fargo in search of a notary. When I arrived at the bank, I asked for Ravin's new boyfriend, Armando. I wanted him to be the one who notarized our paperwork. In addition, I felt as though we needed to talk about some things because I was still wondering when their affair started. It was time for me to face some realities, and I was prepared to meet the man who had a hand in changing the direction in my life—whether it was for better or worse. I knew he worked at the Wells Fargo downtown office at one time or another because a close friend had provided me with the information that the office was conveniently located near Ravin's downtown office. Unfortunately, I was notified the mortgage department had recently moved from the downtown office, and the agent informed me Armando no longer worked in the building.

Soon, a notary appeared and I signed the paperwork under his guidance. When I finished, I called Ravin and told him to meet me on the first floor of his office building as I had the paperwork notarized with my signature. To his surprise, this process took a total of 15 minutes. Ravin came down to meet me and walked me out of the building. He must have been fixated on my weight loss because he told me I was going to have to buy new clothes. I agreed and nodded my head.

As I was preparing to leave, Ravin said, "I love you, Richard!"

I reached out and gave him a hug and left. It was the most empowering day of my life. Although Ravin had a lot of nerve serving me divorce papers after only a month of separation, I pushed through this experience with bravery and recognized I was going to be just fine!

Moving forward, I went back to being a principal that December 8th afternoon. Believe it or not, I felt a sense of relief. Signing the divorce papers was behind me. I felt brave standing up to Ravin with confidence. Deep down, I felt he was questioning his decision to leave. And if I were wrong, I could only wish him much happiness. It was time to focus on me again, and I became a mad writer.

Focusing on research, I finished collecting data from my study on differentiated instruction, and I was trying to make sense of the overwhelming number of sources collected. Then I had started working out twice a day. Moving forward every day, I put anywhere from one to two hours aside for writing. I read other dissertations so I could determine exactly what my next chapter should look like as I shared results from my study. When I woke up each morning on the weekends, I went on a five-mile run. I signed up for another marathon to give me motivation. I did not want any time to think about the divorce, which would have distracted me drastically.

Even though I did not have enough time to train, I felt comfortable knowing I trained at least five miles per day and had the right mindset to complete the marathon. During weekends, I would write when I returned from the five-mile jog. I would set a timer and sit at the computer while making sense of the data and putting it into context based on my school's context. If I experienced writer's block, I would spend only an hour writing and return to the research later in the evening. Usually, I completed a second workout in the evening. This involved a shorter jog and some weight training.

After evening workouts, I cooked dinner and sipped on a glass of wine. Afterward, I would sit at the laptop (still sipping that same glass of wine) focusing on data analysis and continuing to write my next chapter. When I was feeling lonely, I went to the nearby coffee shop to write so that I would be surrounded by people. These strategies were working really well for me, and I experienced progress. I became obsessed with completion. I felt like an angry writer, doing whatever it took to complete the chapter before me. Struggling with an array of emotions, I channeled all my energy toward the finish.

During the week, I arrived early at Star View STEM Academy, usually at 5:00 AM. This was time reserved for writing before serving as principal. It worked out perfectly, writing while my mind was fresh and awake. I found I was at my best in the morning before starting my job in the school community. Therefore, I had the evenings to work out, write some more, and mentally prepare for each week day. In addition, I was going to a night class on Wednesdays, meeting with my Learning Support Council (LSC) to prepare for the upcoming dissertation defense in March. Although Ravin had a lot of nerve serving me divorce documents in the midst of a storm, I was in a race to finish on time. In addition, I got a lot of satisfaction knowing Ravin had noticed my haircut, body transformation, and renewed sense of confidence during our downtown meeting. This experience alone made the storm perfect, and I became laser focused.

CHAPTER 7
CHRISTMAS HOST

HOSTING A CHRISTMAS CELEBRATION WAS ANOTHER tradition that changed. Every year, Ravin and I had made breakfast for our families. It was a way to gather both sides of the family in fellowship. This was considered a ritual for our families over our eight-year relationship. Although the house felt empty after Ravin left, I decided to move forward by hosting our families on Christmas Day. It was not fair to exclude anyone from our annual gift exchange, especially our nephew on his side of the family. Therefore, I invited Ravin's mother, nephew, sister, and best friend. I did not want it to be awkward; I just felt as though we should all move forward traditionally. Believe it or not, I also felt that events like this were helping me heal inside. Having people around sealed the gap I was feeling from separation in my heart.

My family also joined in the Christmas Day breakfast. My mom, brothers and their extended families, and friends Tracy and Sandra attended the annual event, too. Together, we ate eggs, tamales, fried potatoes, and pancakes. We shared stories from the year, laughed about our missteps, and discussed the future. Although my soon-to-be "former mother-in-law" was present, none of the conversation was uncomfortable. I had known her for eight years, and I felt like she was part of my family.

Before digging into our Christmas meal, I read a poem to commence breakfast. Referencing the current circumstances, I used this opportunity to share a message with family and friends that I was healing and showing signs of growth, especially after the Thanksgiving prayer delivered a month earlier. I read the poem below in its entirety once everyone was served and sitting at the table.

> *The Voice Within*
> When the door closed,
> I was full of despair.
> I sat and pondered awhile,
> I saw the pieces in a pile.
> The load was heavy,
> And my heart felt weak.
> Suddenly, I heard a voice within,
> Get up my friend remember where you've
>   been.
> You are on a journey,
> I have been here all along.
> Walk ahead, see the next door.

I have a plan, there is more in store.
With fear, I walked to the door.
Pushing hard, I noticed my strength.
It all came back in an instant,
I heard my heart beat, it was no longer
    distant.
As the door opened,
I witnessed all the splendor.
People were laughing with joy.
Happiness for every girl and boy.
I walked through the door,
Overwhelmed by all the love.
I recognized all the faces too.
Come to think of it, it was you.
I am grateful for every one of you!
Thank you for sharing this Christmas Day.
Took me awhile to notice you never left.
But, you made 2017 the absolute best!

We began eating and joined each other in conversation and laughter. At the completion of breakfast, we sorted the gifts by each person's name for whom the presents were intended. This was a tradition Ravin and I used to take part in together. I still enjoy hosting and sharing a home-cooked meal with family and friends as often as possible. For me, making other people happy has always been my intention.

It is also tradition to buy every special person in my life memorabilia from ASU. This has been my way of showing how grateful I am to be given a chance to attend ASU. With a simple gift, I have been able to share that pride with others. I always wanted others to be showered in maroon and gold because this institution of higher education has provided me with so many opportunities. I am forever grateful to the faculty and many colleagues I have met throughout this educational journey.

While opening gifts, we shined the spotlight on each person and waited patiently for a turn. When the last person opened gifts, we quickly changed into our new ASU gear for a family photo. I always loved this activity, and regardless of the circumstances, this year was no different than the past. We went to the front of the house to capture our traditional group photo. The experience was captivating as we continued the photo session in the front yard celebrating our new apparel, striking as many poses as possible. We laughed at one another and shared photos using Apple Airdrop to ensure we shared the best images for social media posts.

This was exactly what I needed to soothe my soul from loss. I enjoyed every part of this Christmas Day experience. I felt no regrets for hosting both sides of the family, mine and Ravin's. Everything worked out perfectly.

Thinking about the remainder of the day, I did not want the time to end because I knew I would be alone again. Hosting this Christmas breakfast was another huge success and a leap forward. Although I knew the morning could not last forever, I moved on to focusing on the continuation of writing the next chapter of my dissertation. In addition, as the Christmas host, I felt even more love than I had before breakfast. For that, I wrote with gratitude.

CHAPTER 8
MEETING PEOPLE

Although life was busy, I was still feeling empty, especially at night once the lights went out. My body still felt like it was on fire and I hurt all over. It was common for me to toss and turn before falling asleep. By this time, I was taking the antidepressant, but I still felt loss along with isolation in the dark. Those were the times I really felt fearful. Thankfully, social media kept me feeling hopeful, and I was meeting people and sharing exchanges online. I connected with people who were going through similar ordeals as well as others who were willing to share stories.

One mid-December day, I met another Ravin on Facebook, Justin Ravin. Although his middle name was Ravin, I had many encounters with people associated with this particular name and sometimes these affairs were intimate. I have encountered many Ravin's in my lifetime, including Ravin McCue, Ravin Bridges, Ravin Mariposa, Ravin Charleston, Ravin Rivera, and now Justin Ravin. When Justin Ravin sent me a friend request on Facebook, I started liking his past posts and photos. I chuckled because I am like a magnet to this name. Being new friends online, I viewed his profile and noticed he was a cute younger man. So, I reached out to him and shared my thoughts. In addition, I asked if he would like to go out for dinner sometime so we could get to know each other better. Knowing this was much too soon as I was dealing with traumatic loss, I felt a need to force myself in this direction. I was still torn inside, but I had a strong desire to meet and connect with people.

Justin Ravin agreed to meet and soon he sent his phone number my way. We exchanged text messages and decided to meet for dinner. I was not looking for any long-term relationship; instead, this served as another distraction. Justin Ravin was a beautiful man, and I was looking for someone to spend quality time with so I could overcome the feelings of despair. As I took a breather from exercising and writing my dissertation, I needed to fill those down moments, and this was the perfect alternative.

Justin Ravin and I went on a first date in late December. He chose the restaurant P.F. Changs, which probably was not my first choice, but I went along for the adventure. I arrived first, and some confusion about the meeting made things a little awkward initially. I was waiting for him to arrive inside the building, while he was waiting for me outside. For a second, as the time ticked away, I thought he might have stood me up. Eventually, we found each other. As I peered out the glass window of the restaurant, I saw a man checking his watch as well, possibly thinking I may have him stood up.

Finally meeting in person, I found Justin Ravin to be really cute. He was short, and right off the bat, I noticed he had small, feminine hands. Based on my first impression, I was not sure whether I was going to like him all that much, but I braced myself and maintained an open mind. After dinner at P.F. Changs, we went to the movies and watched a gay film at the Camelview Theater at Scottsdale Fashion Square Mall. We held hands, and it actually felt good to be in this kind of space with someone again, although it was way too early for me emotionally. After the movies, we went to the Shake Shack and enjoyed milkshakes. We drove to my house and enjoyed an intimate kiss. It was nothing more than an exchange on the lips because I definitely was not ready for more. We planned to get together again sometime soon as we were nearing the holidays, but that was the end of that night.

Later, we put another date night together for New Year's Eve. We decided to meet in downtown Chandler to ring in the New Year together. I had never hung out in this area, so it was a first for me. Being a native of the area, Justin Ravin named the restaurant. I was tired that night but did what it took to drag myself out of the house. I needed this type of distraction as I was not going to sit at home and dwell on past experiences. I met him at the restaurant and things started to get a little awkward quickly. It obviously was a straight, conservative restaurant, and I felt a lot of close-minded people around me, definitely not my choice for a meeting spot. Generally, I surround myself with people who are liberal and open-minded. To say the least, I felt like a fish out of water.

During conversation that night, Justin Ravin asked me about my past. I told him I had been married for a couple of years, and I was getting a divorce. He asked me how long since the break-up and I told him the truth, late October. His immediate response was that I was dating way too soon and October was not that long ago. I informed him that was for me to decide, although I knew he was right. After dinner, we drove around the area and he pointed out his elementary, middle, and high school he attended. In addition, he pointed out the apartment complex in which he lived. We returned to the restaurant parking lot just as the New Year approached. As the clock struck 12:00, we kissed passionately through the change from one year to the next. It was sweet, and we said goodnight, going our separate ways.

Moving onward, we talked on the phone a few more times and he committed to cheer me on at the Rock 'n Roll Marathon I was running on Martin Luther King Jr. weekend. I asked him to meet me at the finish line because I thought that would be romantic. He agreed and we talked up until that weekend. On the day of the race, I was under the impression he would be there because our last conversation ended assuring me that would be the case. Because I am a person of truth, I expect others to be of the same character trait. I texted him throughout the race to let him know my projected finish time. I never heard back from him after any of those text messages. No problem, I thought, he must have been busy. The race was long and hard, but I finished.

As I crossed the finish line, I looked for Justin Ravin, but I did not see him anywhere in sight. He was not to be found. We also planned to get dinner that evening so I called him and left several messages. When he did not answer, things started to appear a bit peculiar. So I looked him up on Facebook and Instagram to send him a private message; however, I could no longer find him on social media. Suddenly, it dawned on me that when I was calling him by phone, I was getting his voice message greeting without a ring. Therefore, I discovered he had blocked me by phone, Facebook, and Instagram.

Experiencing this behavior, I felt badly for him. I could not understand why he felt like he had to choose this method to lose contact. I wondered why he could not tell me he was not interested. Perhaps we could have been friends, even if he was scared to date someone just leaving a marriage. I was in the middle of crisis, and that was not an easy fact to swallow after all I already had gone through. People behave differently, however, and I could not own his actions. I had to move on from this moment, too.

In January, I met another young man named Andy Jordy. After working out at Results Only Fitness in midtown one morning, I was on my way to work. Before getting on the freeway, I stopped at Lux Coffee on Central Avenue in downtown Phoenix. I parked in the first available parking space in the dark. As I was getting out of my car and crossing the parking area to enter Lux, I saw a gray Nissan Altima pulling into the parking lot from Central Avenue like a maniac. It appeared like the driver was almost out of control. Because I was in the first parking space, I was right near the entrance off the street. I was just about clear from the driveway when this driver nearly hit me with his car while I was on foot. I scurried out of his way and gave him a slowdown hand signal. I continued on my way to Lux to get in line for coffee.

Inside Lux, I ordered and was waiting for my coffee at the counter. As I was facing the employees, someone from behind tapped my shoulder. I turned around and a young man with red hair and a brown beard was standing a few inches from my face.

Invading my space, he said, "Sorry for almost hitting you in the parking lot."

I responded, "That was you? You are a crazy driver. You really should use a little more caution in the parking lot." I could tell by his reaction he was surprised I made this statement. I continued boldly, "Just for that, you owe me coffee some time and we should exchange numbers."

We introduced ourselves and I learned his name was Andy Jordy. During the exchange of numbers, I thought nothing of it until I received a text message later in the day. In the message, Andy shared it was nice to meet. Returning his text, I shared with him that we should get together sometime for coffee. He agreed, but informed me he was headed to Shanghai, China, for a break and he would be back sometime in mid-January. I told him to get in touch with me when he returned, and we eventually would meet up for coffee. If anything, I thought I had met a new friend, and at this point in my journey, meeting people was all I needed.

CHAPTER 9
AFTER MARATHON WEEKEND

For three months, I had trained for the marathon that took place on Martin Luther King Jr. weekend in 2018. Although I had been jogging daily, I never ran more than five miles. Sometimes, I ran twice a day and worked on speed, which I figured would help with longevity. Also, my trainer, Joshua Mendez, helped prepare me for the marathon as our morning workouts became even more intense. These workouts included 40 minutes of strength training alongside cardiovascular conditioning, including tumbling, speed boxing, and running through obstacle courses. Although 5:00 AM was early morning, he mixed up the workouts so they were fun, exciting, and something I anticipated.

In addition to training, dating was casual. I really thought Justin Ravin was going to meet me at the finish line. That was somewhat of a motivation to complete the race. When he committed to being there, I did not even consider that he was going to flake out. I trusted his word.

The day of the race arrived and I text messaged him at the start line to let him know I was about to begin. From the onset, this race was challenging. Around the 16th mile, I hit a wall and struggled from that point forward. I was determined to finish so I pushed myself, putting one foot in front of the other. I struggled and looked forward to seeing Justin Ravin at the end of the race. As I crossed the finished line, I could see family and friends waiting for me at the other side of the finish line. Unfortunately, I never saw Justin Ravin.

Suddenly, my legs started to cramp up like I never felt before. Luckily, my friend Sara and her son Corbi were there to catch me. I was able to use Sara's shoulder to brace myself while I worked through the cramp. Even though I had to swivel my ankle by the ball of my foot, when the rest of my family arrived, I was able to celebrate the finish with them.

When I recognized Justin Ravin blocked me from any contact with him, I was disappointed in Justin because he was unable to be honest. Simply sharing that he was not interested in continuing to see each other was all I expected. To me, it would have been an easy conversation because we were not as emotionally connected in this developing relationship. I shrugged it off and put the responsibility on him. He must have had some insecurity that he was not able to communicate his intentions. Blocking me seemed really immature, and I decided to move forward.

Toward the end of January, work on my dissertation really started to stack up. I was finishing the results section and also beginning the concluding section to my dissertation. In addition, I had started seeing Andy Jordy more frequently. It seemed like a fresh start, and he was a really nice guy. I was attending ASU basketball games regularly, And Andy went with me to a few basketball games. But it all felt like a distraction to the pain and loss I was feeling from my marriage.

One day, Andy and I went to the university early and walked around. It was a refreshing experience. Andy was a photographer, so we took a few pictures while on campus. One of my favorite photos was an image of me walking over the University Bridge by the Palo Verde dormitories. Andy had suddenly asked me to stop and turn around while I was crossing the bridge as he waited at the base. He snapped a shot of me standing on the steps with blue skies overhead with my signature "forks up" signal while using both hands. The color contrast in the photo was aesthetically pleasing to the eye. I believe Andy digitally enhanced the color even more using some photo apps. Anyhow, the whole experience was enjoyable because it was extraordinarily different.

By late afternoon, we attended the game and the Devils won. The team was doing well under head coach Bobby Hurley. The team had a lot of talent and energy. Again, I enjoyed going to the games as a distractor to the real life turmoil I was experiencing inside. Dating Andy, going to the games, and writing my dissertation were ways I diverted my attention from all the change occurring in my life.

Soon afterward, I started staying the night at Andy's apartment more frequently. He lived in a high-rise condominium near Camelback Road and Central Avenue in Midtown Phoenix. The view of North Phoenix was absolutely astounding from his place. Every time I stayed at Andy's, I felt like I was perched in the sky, secluded from the lies and deception occurring on the streets below. It was a great escape. Although I was staying at Andy's, I never had the appetite for sex. I just wanted nothing to do with him sexually. I only wanted a sleeping companion to soothe some of the darkness I was feeling. I recognize that was not fair to him, but that was where I was emotionally at that moment.

Naturally, Andy and I would get intimate at times, rubbing up against one another. We never shared any sexual penetration and simply masturbated in each other's company. I did not know how long this was going to last. Most mornings when I stayed over, I woke up around 4:30 AM to work out with Joshua. The new workouts and changes to my body had me inspired more than ever. If I were not working out with Joshua, I was going to the first Results Only workout class at 5:30 AM. All of these activities, including workouts, marathon training, dating, and writing my dissertation, were distractions. I could see my body changing, so I made the most of each experience. This was a busy time in my life as I was moving closer to completing my dissertation and preparing for the defense. In addition, I still had night classes and continued waiting for my divorce to drop at any second. I felt fortunate to have Andy by my side knowing life was about to shift emotionally again once I received paperwork from the court finalizing my divorce.

CHAPTER 10
DIVORCE IS FINAL

A COUPLE OF DAYS BEFORE VALENTINE'S DAY, PAPER-work arrived in the mail from Maricopa County Courts. I did not open the envelope because I knew the contents. My divorce was final somewhere around February 9; I did not need to open the mail as a reminder to the nightmare I was experiencing. Although I had been waiting for this to finalize, I still was not prepared for the emotional toll it was taking on my mind, body, and spirit, not to mention, my now-ex-husband had been posting photos of himself and Armando Wakefield as a couple on social media, including on Facebook and Instagram. Although Ravin had unfriended me on both social media sites, the first time I noticed a photo of the newer couple was on Instagram in early February. Seeing these images for the first time made my body go numb. My heart felt pierced by a sharp object. I did not feel as though this was classy or tasteful. People began to call and rally behind me with support. My friends felt

I had been betrayed as they reached out frequently to ensure I was stable.

In addition, our mutual friends could see what was occurring and checked on my well-being as it appeared to be taking an emotional toll on my appearance. Some friends considered unfriending Ravin on social media as a result of his postings about his new relationship. I could not understand Ravin's intentions because we had vowed not to unfriend one another on social media and to be civil if we had problems in our relationship. I committed to this agreement and was cautious about posting anything that might hurt Ravin. I understood that he chose to be in a new relationship before ours was officially over, but posting pictures before our divorce was in nobody's best interest.

From a perspective of class and tastefulness, the energy you give off is the energy you get back. How could anything good for Ravin come from these posts? Everyone who knew the two of us as a married couple knew that he left our relationship to be in another without any time in between. The question that surfaced from many of our friends was, "How can he be emotionally ready for another relationship without time to overcome the last?" To me, it appeared to be too soon. I had to throw myself into my work and had distracted myself by spending time with Andy.

Consequently, I informed Andy of the divorce and the finality of my relationship with Ravin. To me, the best virtue in friendship or relationship is to be honest.

We decided to celebrate this closure on Valentine's Day. I had flowers delivered to Andy's condominium. Andrew invited me to go to dinner at his favorite Chinese restaurant on Camelback. I arrived at Andy's condominium and we walked to the Chinese restaurant, which was across the street near his place. I appeared to be together on the outside, but internally I was an emotional wreck. I put on a happy face and Andy again snapped a photo while I was eating at the table. It was the first smile the world had seen on my face in a while. I had hope that brighter days were on the horizon.

Although I had not developed any deep feelings for Andy, I was taking steps forward, which was critical to more healing. I still felt really badly that it was at Andy's emotional expense. I could see that he was falling for me, and I felt as though I should control the pace in which our relationship was moving. Therefore, I was dedicated to honesty.

Ravin, in contrast, had no idea what his actions were doing. He sent me a text message in late February asking if he could come over and look for a suit jacket he left behind in the house we shared together. I did not respond to his text initially. I was not prepared to see him at that moment. I felt as though every time I saw Ravin, it opened a new wound and set me back a few paces. Therefore, I felt it was best to just ignore his text responses. Although I received divorce paperwork, I felt a sense of balance with focusing on work, exercising with Josh, taking an antidepressant, seeing a psychotherapist regularly, writing my dissertation, and preparing for the defense. Seeing Andy on top of it was a bit overwhelming.

Life appeared to be moving along quickly and all of these pieces were coming together like a jigsaw puzzle. Replying to Ravin and letting him into the house would have been like pouring salt over an open wound in my heart. I just could not bring myself to respond to his text message just yet. Although the divorce was final on paper, I was not quite done emotionally.

CHAPTER 11
TIME TO DEFEND

M ARCH WAS A BUSY MONTH. I CHOSE MARCH 30 AS the date to defend my dissertation. I was the second to defend of the five members on my LSC. The dissertation was due in final draft to my committee by March 18 to provide each member enough time to read the work and prepare questions for the defense. The month was intense, to say the least. I also had to deliver a practice defense in front of my LSC peers two nights before on March 28.

I spent the month writing final pieces and preparing my PowerPoint for defense day. To say I was busy is an understatement. Seeing the light at the end of the tunnel was keeping my flame from dimming. During the month, I found out my Aunt Lorraine had a second bout with cancer. It was stage 4 ovarian cancer that had spread to other areas of her body, including her liver, stomach, and throat. I was devastated by this new development, but I had to push it to the back of my mind. I had to frame her prognosis differently; otherwise, I was going to become distracted from finishing my research. Therefore, I began to use the experience as another form of motivation. I had already been through so much. I was now working to complete my defense in honor of my Aunt Lorraine. I had come this far, I was not going to stop at this point.

After spending some time in the hospital, my Aunt Lorraine had returned home and had chosen not to have visitors. I was not permitted to see her for the time being; therefore, I remained focused on completing my PowerPoint presentation, meeting the deadline to submit my dissertation, attending my last ASU class, and preparing for delivery on March 30.

I invited my family to attend the defense and the stage was set. There to support me were my mother, brothers Gabriel and Anthony, sister-in-law Stacey, and my longtime friend Pam Duty. I invited Pam because she had read every rough draft of my dissertation; therefore, I wanted her to be a part of this experience. March 30 came and I delivered what I felt like was a stellar performance considering the circumstances. I took every question asked by my committee, which was made up of Dr. Kim, Dr. Whitmarsh, Dr. McKenzie, and Dr. Myers. I provided responses based on the evidence written in my study. After devoting numerous hours reviewing my research and studying the collection of data, I successfully defended my action research by answering all questions satisfactorily. For the first time in my life,

I felt proud of this three-year project I had worked so diligently to complete. I recalled all of my research thoroughly and finally made it through the adversity I had endured over the past five months. While the committee discussed my defense practices, I was asked to leave the room along with my guests to determine how the committee would proceed. Although we all waited anxiously in the lobby for the outcome, I felt confident I had passed the defense process.

Waiting in the lobby seemed like a lifetime as I watched the minutes go by with my friends and family. After the committee deliberated and came to a conclusion, I was brought back into the room alongside my guests. I sat in front of the committee as they began to share recommendations to add to my study. First, they wanted me to add a definition of design thinking, which was a model to support student group work. Second, I was asked to explain "Gradual Release of Responsibility" because it was a learning structure used to support teachers in differentiated instruction. Third, the committee wanted me to explain how I was going to use this with my colleagues in future educational experiences. Finally, the committee wanted me to explicitly describe how I would replicate the study in my context during the upcoming school year. I felt as though all these recommendations were manageable. In addition, they would keep me occupied until the dissertation was due again during the first week of May. Once all of the recommendations were made by the committee, Dr. Kim said, "Congratulations, Dr. Ramos! With these changes, we declare you a doctoral graduate." My heart leapt with joy and my family smiled. I passed my defense and I was on my way to graduation. Moreover, I was a single man again and free to explore all of life's possibilities. For me, it signified a huge victory after five extremely challenging months.

April was another busy month. I was glad to have the dissertation defense behind me by this time. With the additions I needed to make to my dissertation, I felt at ease with the list of recommendations by the committee. Some of the components had been written in previous rough drafts, and I just needed to locate the writing and make refinements to support the final draft. Once all of the content was updated, I was content with the final product and I submitted my action research to the committee for the final time.

Although I had unfinished work to complete, it was time to turn my attention to celebrations and graduations. I continued seeing my psychotherapist during this time. I shared my accomplishments of completing my dissertation defense. My therapist was surprised and impressed I was able to finish collecting data, writing chapters, and defending my work with the personal trauma that had taken place during the semester. We focused on those accomplishments during my April session. At this point, I was seeing my therapist just once a month as I had scaled back tremendously because I could feel I was healing.

During my April session, I shared my feelings about Andy Jordy. I found him to be a really nice guy, but I was not feeling love. It was a new adventure, and I was just having fun exploring other people. We were watching ASU basketball games, trying various restaurants, and staying the night together at his condo frequently. Also, I enjoyed sleeping with a warm body again. My therapist advised me to continue having fun but to be honest with Andy. My therapist still expected I would get angry about my divorce at some point, but I just was not feeling that way. Anger was definitely not the way I would describe how I felt. Instead, I felt more hurt and betrayal than anger. Besides, I had too many other distractions in life, and I was moving forward.

As an LSC, our chair Dr. Kim took all five doctoral graduates to dinner to celebrate our dissertation defense accomplishments at Gen Korean BBQ at Tempe Marketplace. All four of my colleagues passed the defense, and therefore, the five of us joined Dr. Kim. It was an enjoyable first-time experience in a stress-free atmosphere. No one had anxiety any longer with our dissertation defenses behind us. The conversation was exhilarating, and we enjoyed one another's company in this new setting. Including Dr. Kim, six doctors were now at the table. It was a great way to celebrate the effort, dedication, and hard work of the past three years.

April was eventful, and the next activity of the month was an especially big one. My little brother Gabriel graduated from Grand Canyon University (GCU) with a bachelor of art's degree in special education. This was a huge celebration because Gabriel had accomplished this task as a middle-age man raising a family of five. He did his student teaching in the same district where I served as a principal. Because teachers were in high demand, the district paid him while he student-taught throughout the year. His graduation was a huge leap forward for him and his family. I was proud of his accomplishments.

Although I my research day was scheduled on his graduation date, I was able to step away and attend his graduation in the GCU Activity Center. Research day was one of the final requirements to complete my degree. This project was an online forum in which every doctoral student participated to share his or her progress on action research. I received permission from GCU's administration to participate on site so that I could attend my brother's commencement exercises in the afternoon. I arrived at the GCU Arena at 1:00 PM to attend graduation. I was ecstatic for my brother and his efforts. I could not imagine how difficult it must have been to complete a degree while raising a family and working. The ceremony was incredible and an important family event.

Aunt Lorraine did not attend because she was already starting to feel exhausted because of the cancer. With her absence, I knew her prognosis was severe. If she were healthy, she would have been in attendance. Aunt Lorraine always understood the significance of big events, especially college graduation. She never missed an event of this magnitude.

After my brother's graduation from GCU, I attended a graduation party in honor of Gabriel that evening. The gathering was in his home backyard. Tables were set, family arrived, food was served, and friends congregated to celebrate my brother's accomplishment. It was a great way to honor my brother for his dedication to education and family. It also marked the start of his teaching journey, a career that we both are so passionate about, especially as we get the opportunity to positively influence the lives of our youth.

CHAPTER 12
GRADUATION

MAY WAS NOTHING MORE THAN A CELEBRATORY MONTH. At the month's start, I celebrated my 46th birthday on Thursday, May 3. In addition, I participated in three graduations beginning with general ASU commencement on May 7; teacher's college commencement on May 11; and Latino convocation on May 12. For me, it was important to participate in all three ceremonies because it marked the last time I would be attending classes at the university. As far as higher education is concerned, earning a doctorate was a dream come true. Therefore, I savored the moment and enjoyed the experience of all three commencements. In addition, it gave family and friends a chance to attend one of three ceremonies based on busy schedules. As a result, my family and best friends like my cousin Mike and best friend Melody were able to attend at least one of the commencement exercises.

Although, it was great to have friends and family attend the ceremonies, my Aunt Lorraine was not able to make it to any of them. Before she had been diagnosed with stage 4 cancer, she had attended all of my past graduations. Aunt Lorraine was such a significant supporter of my educational career, so for her not to be present was difficult for me. When she did not arrive at any of the commencement ceremonies, I recognized even more so the severity of her diagnosis. Knowing her over my lifetime, she would not have missed this event for the world. Aunt Lorraine was there at the outset of my college career. She offered me a place to live in the beginning when I attended ASU as freshman in 1990. Had she been feeling well, she never would have missed my doctoral graduation. During each ceremony, I looked for her in the crowd just hoping she would arrive, but she never showed. I have never hated cancer so much as I did during each of these ceremonies. Cancer had a hold on my Aunt Lorraine, and she was unable to see the culmination of the journey we started together.

The Latino convocation was my favorite. It was a cultural experience with a Latin flavor, including folkloric dancers and Spanish announcers. It set the mood for the celebration that was to come afterward at my house. Like Gabe's graduation party, I invited the most important people in my life to celebrate this accomplishment. This was a milestone in my life, because the doctoral program was so rigorous and life had been so difficult over that five-month period. To finish the process was the most rewarding experience. And, I wanted the most important people in my life there to share the moment with me.

Figure 1. Richard Ramos with Uncle Ray Ramos.

One guest who arrived to the party, whom I was so pleased to see, was my Uncle Ray Ramos.

He brought along his lovely wife Aunt Sandy, and I felt so much gratitude for their participation. Uncle Ray had been supporting me through my youth, education and career, marriage equality, and now my doctoral studies. It was so important for him to attend. During the party, I did not recognize that it was even more critical for him to be there because his days on Earth were limited. None of us had a clue as to what was about to happen. Like Aunt Lorraine, Uncle Ray was devoted and always showed up to important family affairs. It was as if he had this intuitive sense and supported others at just the right moment. It was so good to celebrate with him and Aunt Sandy.

May was a tough month as well. I called things off with Andy Jordy at the beginning of the month. Andy's expectations of me grew and his demands were becoming overwhelming. The beginning of May was a busy month, and I was not able to meet with him often or spend the night at his condo. Between his regular alcoholic anonymous (AA) meetings, our jobs, and busy schedules, we were just not able to connect. Our final interaction was disappointing, unfortunately, so I moved on without him.

Andy and I were supposed to go to breakfast tentatively on April 29. By the time I woke and text messaged Andy, he was already out to breakfast with a friend. I did not have an issue with that and informed him I would connect with him later. I called him later that morning and I believe he was at an AA meeting. I text messaged him asking to save some time for dinner later. As for me, I was not having a problem that we were missing each other, as I was really self-sufficient. So I went to the gym and exercised for the day, which included an outdoor run. Around 4:30 PM, I text messaged Andy to let him know that I was incredibly hungry and I was ready to eat. For 30 minutes, I waited for a response from Andy and when I did not get one back, I went to a hamburger restaurant close by for dinner. After ordering and sitting in a booth waiting on my order, Andy finally text messaged me at 5:15 PM and asked me what I would like to do for dinner. I told him in a text message I was already at a restaurant because I did not hear back from him. Andy became irate and the text messages quickly turned negative. He told me my actions spoke loudly: he did not feel important and that I was self-serving.

Actually, I felt the complete opposite, but I did not have the energy to exchange distasteful text messages. So I just responded with, "I am sorry." I did not need that type of energy in my life at this time and so I stopped responding. A couple of weeks later, once Gabe's graduation, my birthday, and ASU graduation passed, Andy text messaged me saying I had used my silence as a weapon. He also indicated it was not fair. In all honesty, I did not think his text messages were fair. I used silence to let things pass over, not as a weapon. I did not like our earlier text message exchanges, so I thought time needed to pass for the both of us. Again, I told him I was sorry and felt like I had been misunderstood. I did not have the energy to fight, so I let it go. Besides, I had a lot going on at my job.

In the middle of May, a new movement started in support of teachers. Teachers did not show up for work and protested at the Arizona State Capital. After many years, teachers protested for an increase in pay, not only for themselves, but for classified staff members. Teachers lined the streets of downtown Phoenix in solidarity. Arizona ranked 50th out of 50 states in educational funding, and teachers decided to take action about an increase in funds. They called their movement

#RedForEd. It was powerful and I was proud of the staff I worked alongside. I empowered teachers over the five years I was at the school, so it was not a surprise they were taking the lead to advocate for students, teachers, and classified staff members. I was thrilled to support their advocacy but became concerned when they did not return to school for a total of eight days.

Every day became a guessing game. Some days I thought they would return to work; then, there would be another hurdle at the legislature, so they stayed on the lawn protesting at the capitol for a longer period. Finally, the governor announced he was going to increase teachers' pay and school resumed. Our district decided teachers would have to make up their extra days at the end of the official school year and well past Memorial Day. I was concerned about the additional days added to the calendar because I already had planned a trip to Germany. I was treating myself to this trip for completing my doctorate, and I was taking nine days off to celebrate starting on the Friday before Memorial Day. I thought I was going to have to cancel my trip and accommodate those additional days added to the calendar. I talked to my human resource director about the schedule, and she honored my trip. She told me to take the trip as I had earned the time. Therefore, the assistant principal and dean of students would supervise teachers as they made up the extra days. I felt grateful to work in an understanding district that allowed me to celebrate my hard work in earning a doctorate.

CHAPTER 13
GERMANY

G ERMANY WAS YET ANOTHER DISTRACTION. I WAS going to see my longtime friend Stephan Duerre. I had met Stephan in New York when we were both visiting the city in 2004. I met him at a night club in the city. We entered the restroom at the same time and I noticed his impressive physique. He was also handsome.

After our initial meeting, we became friends. In 2004, he came to the United States to visit me in Arizona. Soon after, I went to Germany to visit that same year. We stayed in touch over time, and here I was returning to Germany for the second time 14 years later. The trip was eventful as I went to a historical hospital museum that treated people with tuberculosis during World War II. I attended a couple of theatrical performances as well. One was under a tent featuring a one-man show who imitated famous singers from around the world. The costumes were made out of flat cardboard material and interchangeable to represent the personality behind each song. Personalities included Cher, Madonna, Lady Gaga, Elvis Presley, and other mega stars. It was really a clever idea for a show. We also took a couple of boat tours: one in Berlin to tour the city, and another that was closer to the border with Poland. The significance of this second tour was that people got around in this particular city by boat only. It was really spectacular. In addition, I visited a few museums, one on the history of the Berlin Wall and another on World War II, and finally, I toured a bunker from the War. It was quite interesting as remnants from the war seemed to dominate the City of Berlin. Also, I went to the Olympic Stadium and read the placards about Germany's history in the world games. Again, I was quite fascinated, especially as a former history major.

One of the most exciting events that took place was Stephan arranged for me to visit an elementary school while I was there. As a principal, I had the opportunity to meet with a German principal, and we discussed the similarities and differences in our school systems. Very quickly, I learned the principal felt as though German schools were inferior because of the lack of technology. I hesitated in telling him that my school was a one-to-one laptop device–to–student school. That might have pushed him over the edge and validated his point. I kept this knowledge to myself and asked questions to discover as much as possible. It was an amazing learning experience.

As for Stephan and me, we had a romantic time. I enjoyed his company, and we dined like we had the first time in New York City. I was a single man, learning to make it on my own. He understood this and had my best interest at heart for nine days. We visited a lot of tourist attractions, but most of all I enjoyed reconnecting with Stephan. I was pretty sure if Stephan lived in the United States, we would be together. Anyhow, Germany was much better this time around, and I would go back to visit anytime.

Once I returned home from Germany, life changed again. I was no longer attending classes or writing a dissertation. It had been more than a month since my defense. I thought things would slow down some. In early June, I went to the Arizona Department of Education Leading Change Conference, which was another distractor. I attended various workshops and exercised at the luxurious Starr Pass Hotel in Tucson, Arizona. My concern started to grow about my Aunt Lorraine's stage 4 cancer diagnosis. I had heard stories about her condition worsening, yet I still was not permitted to see her. I found this odd because we had an amazing relationship. When I asked my mom about her health, she told me things like her health was declining, and she did not want to see anyone right now because it reminded her that she is dying.

If I had the chance to see my aunt, I knew I could brighten her spirits. I started talking to close family members about the possibility of seeing Aunt Lorraine. By mid-June, I had a breakthrough. My Aunt Deb told me that they were having a family sisters' day in late June, and she was supposed to pick up Aunt Lorraine and bring her to the gathering. Aunt Deb asked if I would like to pick her up and transport her to the meeting. This would surprise my Aunt Lorraine, and I would get that chance to see her for myself. I agreed to be the one to take her from her home to see her sisters at my Aunt Deb's place.

I took the morning off from work that day and drove over to my Aunt Lorraine's house in Chandler. I knocked on the door and I could hear the dogs barking from inside. I was flooded with anticipation as my Aunt Lorraine answered the door. She and her partner Sandra answered the door and both were surprised to see me standing outside. Immediately, I was invited inside as we exchanged hugs and kisses. Both ladies expressed how they had not seen me in a long time. They wanted me to sit down and talk for a little before leaving. It was great to see them both and we exchanged small talk. Sandra, Lorraine's longtime partner, told me that I was always welcome back, not to let too much time pass before my next visit. I was confused because my mom had told me Aunt Lorraine did not want to see anyone. If Sandra was inviting me back soon, I wondered how come she did not know that my Aunt Lorraine did not want visitors. Besides, why did I have to sneak my way in to pick her up on this particular day? It just did not make sense to me, especially if I had an open pass to visit their house at any time. Something was not making sense.

Aunt Lorraine and I started our journey to Aunt Deb's house so she could join her sisters and spend time together. We held hands the whole time and talked about how much we missed each other. My Aunt Lorraine repeatedly told me how much she loved me, and she asked if I knew that she was dying. In response, I confirmed I was aware, but I asked her if we could celebrate all the time she had left. This changed the conversation and tears were shed because we knew we had a special gift in our relationship. Together, we were always the life of the parties and family gatherings. Like multipliers, we transferred our light and energy onto others. We were like two peas in a pod. When we walked into the room, we surged with positivity and it permeated. We shared a common bond for we bother were loud, humorous, and free spirited, and we both were vivacious dancers, too. We loved to entertain. Together, we felt safe and the love was mutual. We spent the rest of the car ride to Aunt Deb's holding hands, telling stories, and savoring the moment. It was a special time together.

The month of June was full of surprises. I went to dinner with one of my former teachers, Tony Knowles, the night before he was moving back to Chicago. He had taught at my school for four years. He was an amazing teacher, my confidante, and quite a professional resource. I was going to miss him, so I was glad he made time to meet for dinner before leaving. As I arrived to pick him up, he looked amazing in jeans. I always had a little crush on him but never would I cross the line with a subordinate. Besides, he was leaving for Chicago the very next day.

At dinner, like always, I enjoyed our conversation. On the way home, we spent some time in silence because I knew I would be leaving him at his apartment for the last time. I was not going to see him again for a long period of time. There would be no more daily interactions at school either. It was a bit awkward. I left him off and had no idea what was in store. Tony was leaving the next day, and his dad had arrived to drive back to Chicago with him.

The next day, Tony text messaged me at 8:00 AM to ask if I had time to see him before leaving town. I was at breakfast with my mom at that moment. I looked at my watch, estimated how much time it would take me to finish eating, and responded that I would meet him back at my place at 9:00 AM. My mom and I finished breakfast, and I took her home. Afterward, I went home and waited for Tony to arrive. I anticipated what was about to happen, but I stayed calm.

That crush was mutual. We were going to cross the line, and he was no longer a subordinate. The minute Anthony walked into the house, we kissed passionately and a new journey began. We undressed each other, and I led him to my bedroom. For a good hour, we passionately kissed and simply enjoyed holding one another. It was an amazing feeling, and I knew it was the beginning of something special. Before Anthony left on his journey, I told him I would be seeing him soon in Chicago. My focus shifted again and I started planning.

CHAPTER 14
CHICAGO

WHEN I MAKE A COMMITMENT, I FOLLOW THROUGH. So on July 1, I traveled to Chicago to explore a relationship with Tony Knowles. I was excited; I would be staying in the downtown area for a few nights in the Wrigley Field area in a vacation rental. It was Tony's birthday so I was full of anticipation. It was actually the first time I felt butterflies in my stomach about a possible relationship since being with Ravin. Tony and I were both thrilled to see each other.

I arrived in the early morning, and Tony was coming to meet me later that afternoon. As soon as he arrived, we could not keep our hands away from each other. We made passionate love, celebrated his birthday, and showered together for the first time. It felt nice to be in the presence of this man. We had adored each other for so long, and it felt like we were consummating our friendship. This place felt familiar and inevitable.

Later, we went out to dinner at an Italian restaurant. It was amazing for a variety of reasons. We asked our host to seat us on the balcony so we could overlook the city. We ordered pizza and salad while sharing a bottle of wine. The conversation was relaxing and peaceful. Because we were friends first, it felt comfortable connecting about all our moments in life. It appeared Tony was so happy to be back in Chicago, his hometown. Although I had visited Chicago before, I allowed him to guide our tour. It was his city so I allowed him to take the lead.

Vacation lasted a week, which included spending the July Fourth holiday with friends. In addition, we spent time fellowshipping and exploring the downtown Chicago area. We took pictures and enjoyed one another's company. The relationship appeared to be off to an incredible start.

When I left Chicago, Tony's eyes welled up with tears because we no longer would see each other day to day. The week had gone by so quickly, and we made the most of our experience together. I expressed how important it was to look forward to the next time we would see each other. I told him I would come back soon. I left early morning on Sunday, took the train to the airport, and headed back to Phoenix.

Returning to Phoenix, I had so much work to prepare for at school. New teachers would be arriving soon and beginning professional development by mid-July. School started the last week in July so all the teachers would be back soon, too.

After my arrival in Phoenix, I was busy planning, reading, and organizing for the upcoming school year. I was excited school was starting because it was the first time I did not have to worry about attending classes for my doctoral program, and I felt free like a bird soaring in the wind. I read books like *Mindset: A New Psychology for Success* by Carol Dweck and *Better Learning Through Structured Teaching* by Doug Fisher and Nancy Frey to prepare for the upcoming school year. I designed a long-range plan for professional development and began planning for a *Mindset* book study. The long-range plan was based on replicating my action research study on differentiated instruction to support teachers. I felt like I was in the best place both mentally and emotionally to start school than I had been during my six-year tenure at Star West STEM Academy. I highly anticipated the school year.

One of the events I organized when I returned was the sixth annual neighborhood walk. When all teachers returned the first week, we would once again walk the streets before the start of the school year to remind parents and families about the first day of classes.

We did this event for a number of reasons. One, it built camaraderie among the staff. Two, it was just, plain and simple, good customer service. And most important, it gave teachers the opportunity to see the homes in which our kids live and the surrounding community they come from. Our students came from a multitude of backgrounds, and our teachers need to know whom they served. To effectively teach children, teachers must know the background of each child to nurture those experiences before any learning can take place. Having done this activity in the past, both teachers and family members look forward to this event. It strengthened our image, culture, and trust in the process. It was probably the most important event of the year. It always set us off on the right path. With only a few days to prepare, the start of the school year was met with high anticipation. School spirit was the highest it had ever been. But, I wanted to be in Chicago!

CHAPTER 15
END OF SUMMER

Augusт quickly approached. School was back in session, and this was the month of my brother Anthony's 44th birthday. We gathered at Red Robin to celebrate on August 4. It was a fun time; family and friends came out to the Tempe Market Place to celebrate my brother. The occasion also marked a great way to start out the new month.

As school was getting started, I had a new boss and I was adapting to her leadership style. She came in with a hard-pressed agenda and it appeared she had high expectations. Her name was Crystal Waters, and I had no idea who she was or where she came from. At our first meeting during the month, I recognized she had a perception about Star West and was given the directive to make changes. One of the things she chose to argue about was our design thinking framework for small-group learning. Crystal told me that we were a school of engineering, not design thinking. It angered me because design thinking is engineering. In tandem, the two go together. I had just completed an action research project using the design thinking model; therefore, I knew exactly how the two supported one another. Engineers use design thinking when developing prototypes in their daily work. I defended design thinking, and she did not like that I pushed back.

Another comment she made was that we were not where we needed to be in student achievement. Instead of commending us for passing the state average in seventh-grade English language arts (ELA) and approaching the state average in third grade math as a start, she criticized us for not being where we should be.

I lashed out again and said, "That is not true at some grade levels." I told her about third-grade math and seventh-grade ELA. I could tell she had not done her homework, because she had no idea about the success of these two grade levels. She tried to correct herself by saying we were not there in most grade levels. I was furious about this first coaching session, but I kept my cool.

At this point, I recognized it was going to be a long year with Crystal as my supervisor. Somehow, district officials did not know enough about my school to coach her to focus on the positives first. I am all about meeting expectations and holding high standards, but if you do not notice the good before pointing out the bad, then you lose all credibility with me. It was an interesting start to the year.

By this time, I was no longer taking any medication for depression, nor was I going to any more counseling sessions. I felt strong enough to handle life on my own. I was still dating Tony, and I was headed to Chicago again for a weekend in August. This time, I would be staying in Roseland, Chicago. The anticipation was increasing, and I was excited to explore our relationship further. But first, I had a little distraction.

Suddenly, Ravin had started to text message me during the month of August and wanted to know if his voting ballot had arrived in my mail. After being gone nearly a year, he was still getting large quantities of mail at my house. Through text, I let him know I received his ballot. He then asked if he could pick it up. I responded letting him know I would go home at 4:00 PM, find his ballot, and put it in the mailbox so he could pick it up anytime afterward. I did not want to exchange mail with him in person. Low and behold, I arrived at my house and Ravin was waiting for me, parked on the street in front of my yard.

Instantaneously, I thought, "What kind of game is he playing?"

I did not want nor did I need to see him. I was already being kind enough to leave his ballot in the mailbox for him to pick up. Arriving, I got out of my car and told him I would get the ballot for him.

Ravin had other plans; he followed me into the house and started to look around. He went from room to room. Ravin noticed the remodeling and told me the house looked nice. He went to the back door and peered at the backyard. Ravin made notice that the sugar cane had grown and the pomegranate trees had fruit on them. I told him he did not live there anymore so he should not be looking around the house without permission. I was able to lure him back to the kitchen and out the exit. When outside on the doorstep, I asked him, "Does it feel like home?" Ravin agreed that it sort of did. Without wasting any more time, I told him I was headed out to vote myself, and we should get to the polling place. It all felt really awkward. I saw him when I left the polling place as well. He was outside filling out his ballot before taking it inside. I gave him a hug goodbye and left, thinking that our meeting was very odd.

Later, Ravin and I decided to meet to talk for the first time in late August on Michael Jackson's birthday, August 29. We had so much to talk about, yet we talked about nothing. I had so much to tell Ravin about the way he left our marriage, but I could tell Ravin was distraught. Plus, he looked extremely thin and dreadful. Ravin disclosed things were not going well with his new boyfriend. He told me he almost called me recently because Armando had tossed him up against a wall a week before. I am not sure why he wanted sympathy from me after the way he left our relationship. It was a bizarre meeting. I never shared any of my talking points.

Instead, I tried to be present with my mixed emotions to listen and support Ravin. I wondered why Ravin thought about calling me when he was being physically assaulted by Armando. It did not make sense to me, other than he thought I could save him again. I did not have the energy to save him. I had done that one too many times in our past. This time, he had to be on his own, especially after his handling to the end of our relationship. Ravin looked fearful with gaunt-looking skin as well.

After telling me his story, Ravin told me not to find Armando and start anything with him. I thought to myself, "Don't flatter yourself, I wouldn't dare." Something told me that is exactly what he wanted me to do. But, Ravin was not my husband anymore; therefore, I clearly understood that was no longer my place. One of the things I learned during our meeting was that Ravin planned this meeting for 5:00 PM because Armando was still working or occupied. He also had to be done at a certain time to meet Armando once he finished our meeting. I do not think Ravin recognized I knew that Armando did not know about our meeting. Like in the past, Ravin was being sneaky behind his new partner's back. It was a little awkward but I made it out of that scenario.

As we were saying goodbye, I provided Ravin with a copy of my bound dissertation. I had written most of it while we were married and he had asked to see the outcome. He was happy to receive it and asked if he could keep it. I told him I wanted it back because it was one of two copies bound. To this day, I still have not received that copy back. This is weird. Why would he want to keep something of mine if he was in love with someone else? Perhaps because he never wanted our relationship to end or perhaps he was forced. When I went to tell Ravin goodbye, I went to kiss him. To me, this was nothing extraordinary, for I kiss all of my exes. Ravin turned to the side of his face and said we could not do that because he was in relationship. He was sending all kinds of mixed messages that day, and I did not have time for games. I felt as though this whole meeting was a mess.

Not long after our first meeting, I was sitting on my couch in my underwear at home after a long workday. I unexpectedly received a phone call from Ravin. I contemplated whether or not to answer it, but decided I should do so after our last conversation. Perhaps he needed something. As I answered the phone, Ravin informed me that he was in my front yard and asked if he could come in for a glass of water. I asked him to wait a moment so I could get some clothes on before opening the door. I wondered why he would choose to get water at my house when I lived walking distance to a Fry's Food Store. When I answered the door, he came inside and looked around the house. Ravin retrieved a bottle of water from the refrigerator. Finally, Ravin began telling me that he and Armando were fighting again. I was sitting on the couch in the living room and just listened without comment. I was not sure what he wanted me to do or say about his relationship so I just resorted to silence. Not getting the response he desired, it didn't take long for him to recognize I was not interested so he decided to leave. I walked him to the door and ushered him outside. I was perplexed and had no idea what he expected of me as his ex-husband.

About a week later, I was driving to work at 6:30 AM. I rolled out the driveway and headed down the street to Thomas Road, less than a quarter mile from my house. As I turned onto Thomas, I pulled up to a red stoplight and turned to my right. In disbelief, I noticed Ravin and Armando in the car next to me. They were both in gym clothing as they were coming from the CrossFit gym near my house. For a brief second, I wondered whether or not I should roll down my window to greet them. Given that their windows were down, I ceased the moment.

I rolled down my window and said, "Good morning, gentleman."

Ravin was driving and both of them turned left to look at me. Surprised, Ravin rolled up his window and sped away as soon as the light turned green. It appeared he could not get away fast enough. He eased left with his blinker on to make the next turn onto Highway 51, but when he saw my blinker as I was also going to make a left, he changed his mind and stayed on the road going straight. I continued on my regular route to work for I was not about to start any trouble. For me, I did what came naturally. I said hello and again had the opportunity to show Armando I was a real person and not just a personality. I could not understand why Ravin was bringing his new boyfriend to my neighborhood to work out when they both lived downtown with plenty of gyms in that area. This was especially odd given that Ravin was at my house just a week prior telling me that he was fighting with his boyfriend once again. I was starting to question his stability and happiness.

Was it time for me to move onward or was it not?

CHAPTER 16
COLD HEARTED

O N AUGUST 31, I RECEIVED YET ANOTHER TEXT MES-sage from Ravin while I was at work. He asked me if I was going to watch the Phoenix Mercury WNBA game in the evening. Given that I was a season ticket holder, I assured him I would be at the game. He told me he might be going because he wanted to see his favorite player Dewanna Bonner compete. I never had liked Dewanna Bonner, and he knew that, so I assumed he was just playing more games. Besides, we had been meeting and talking more through text messaging, and I thought it would be great to see him at the game as well. I sent him a picture of my ticket and asked him to come up and see my family. He never had said goodbye to them after leaving the marriage almost a year prior. Without hesitation, he picked up on this and asked if Gabe and Stacey, my brother and his fiancé, would be at the game. I assured him they would be attending the event.

He responded by saying okay and thanked me for letting him know. Then, he joked with me one more time by letting me know that Taurasi's response to winning a recent basketball game against the Connecticut Sun was legendary. Ravin was referring to the end of the last basketball game where one of the Connecticut Sun players clapped and taunted the Mercury bench. So, when the Mercury eliminated the Sun in three play-off games, Taurasi responded to that player by saying, "Who's clapping now bitch." Ravin again reiterated how he thought this was fabulous.

I went to the basketball game that night at Talking Stick Resort Arena thinking that Ravin would be there and would finally bring some closure for my family. During the day, he never mentioned he was bringing Armando to the game. In addition, the two of them had seats in my line of vision below me and my family. I noticed them during the second quarter. My whole family had already spotted them and were hoping I would not notice. I recognized them and my temperature rose instantaneously. I could not believe Ravin had the audacity to not tell me he was bringing Armando during our text message exchange earlier in the day. Not only that, they sat within eye's view the whole night. If he had shared he was bringing Armando during our day texting, I would have been prepared for this sighting.

Needless to say, I was distracted the rest of the game. I was disappointed because I had been watching the Mercury play for years, and I felt like this was my territory. Ravin knew this and came along many times while dating and married, so to bring his new boyfriend along flabbergasted me. Also, Ravin had told me a year earlier he no longer wanted to go to the Mercury games because they frustrated him by not winning and caused him anxiety. If this was my hobby and he did not enjoy the games, then why would he attend with his boyfriend? It didn't make sense to me. Therefore, the events should not have unfolded this way. It seemed like a cold-hearted thing to do.

At halftime, I went to the restroom as usual. As I walked to the hallway, I could not believe my eyes. Standing in line at the concession stand right outside my section was Armando Wakefield. For the first time, I was going to come face to face with the man who came between me and Ravin and our marriage. At first, I was motionless and did not know what to do. Soon after, I thought, "I am going to introduce myself. This man needs to know that I am a real person with emotions and not just a personality." I walked up to Armando and extended my arm for a handshake.

I said, "Hello, I am Richard Ramos. I have wanted to meet you for a really long time. There is so much we have to talk about. If you can find it in your heart to reach out to me some time, I would really appreciate it. Either get my number from Ravin or reach out to me on social media. It is pretty easy to find me."

I simply walked away and went to the restroom. I was shocked by the exchange. I had been waiting to cross paths with that man since the weekend of October 28, 2017, the first night Ravin did not come home after that concert. I did not know whether he was going to get in touch or not. What I did know, though, was that I shook his hand and he saw me eye to eye. Therefore, he knew I existed and had to acknowledge that I was a real person. The thing I did not know was whether he would take me up on my offer. We had so much to talk about. Only time would tell.

CHAPTER 17
GOFUNDME

Aftwr Ravin's cruel behavior, I turned to September for comfort. Two months had gone by since I had last seen Aunt Lorraine. To me, it appeared like she was hostage in her own home. I heard stories she did not want to see anyone because of the way she looked and her partner Sandra did not want any of her relatives around. For some unknown reason, Sandra did not want our family anywhere near their home. I was not quite sure what that was about as I had a great relationship with both of them. Anyhow, I felt like time was running out and I needed to see Aunt Lorraine. Therefore, I reached out to ask Sandra if I could drop by to visit. In a text message, she agreed and asked me to reach out to Lorraine so I did. Aunt Lorraine and I decided to meet up at 6:00 PM the following week.

A week later, I left school by 4:30 PM to make it to the East Valley where she lived in Gilbert. I knew it was going to take some time to get there at the heart of rush hour traffic. I made it just in time. As I knocked on the door, I wondered what I was going to see when Aunt Lorraine answered the door. To my surprise, other than being hunched over with pain in her stomach, she looked really good. After hearing stories of how bad she felt and not wanting to see anybody, I was shocked to find that she was mobile, answered the door, and invited me into her bedroom.

I was dumbfounded. Aunt Lorraine appeared to be in confinement. She was staying in a guestroom in a house I always had considered to be her own. It was odd to see her in a small, guest bedroom because she was always so proud. Although these were unusual circumstances, I wanted to make the most of our visit, so I lay with her on the bed. As we lay together, my aunt was visibly anxious and distraught. With tears in her eyes, she asked me if I knew she was dying. Following that comment, she asked if I was going to be okay with that situation. These were loaded questions to begin our conversation.

Naturally, I grabbed her hand and assured her that I was aware of the circumstances.

I told her, "Of course I am going to be okay. I have a great relationship with you and I will remember all of the good times. I have to keep your legacy alive and I will be love for others."

I could see that she had so much more to say. She was scared. The next thing she discussed was her finances. She was concerned about her medical bills, credit score, every-day expenses, and living arrangement. I was perplexed she was concerned about all of this and having stage 4 cancer at the same time. Health should be her number one concern. It appeared to me that all of these stresses and anxieties were not helping her situation. It just did not make sense to me why her lifelong partner was not doing something to assure her everything was going to be all right.

Medical expenses were mounting, and by the end of the year, she would no longer have medical insurance. She already had more than $10,000 in medical debt, which her insurance would not cover. She was no longer on payroll from work, so the money in her savings account was all she had left on which to live until she passed away. She was concerned her credit score would drop, and she had worked so hard to maintain good credit over the years. It was eerie to talk about, but it was reality.

Finally, she told me that her living arrangement was not the best. Sandra did not want her to die in her house, so she needed to find a place to live. I listened as she agonized over sharing her experiences. I could see this experience was harming her social and emotional well-being, and I could not imagine having these thoughts near the end of life. To alleviate the pressure, I asked her what I could do to help. I had a $100 in my pocket, which I was already going to leave, but I could see that was not going to be enough. I also offered her a place to stay in my new one-bedroom apartment in Tempe. I had just sold my home and I assured her that she was more than welcome to lodge at my place for as long as necessary. I offered the bedroom and let her know that I would either find another place to live or stay on the couch to assist her when she needed me.

After making these offers, she asked me if I would do her favor. Without knowing what she was about to ask, I agreed because I would do anything to ease her pain and lessen the anxiety. Aunt Lorraine asked me to set up a GoFundMe account on social media. Although I agreed to set up the account, I was reluctant to move forward. I was having an ethical problem with this request. That is not the way I use social media to request my acquaintances donate money. The messages I post are usually positive and uplifting for others to use as motivation. I never post to take anything from anyone. This was a tough decision I had to make, but I agreed to help her in any way possible.

When I left that day, I put the $100 on her dresser. I began to consider how I was going to arrange the GoFundMe account and to whom might I send the request. I was having a hard time with this commitment, but I knew Aunt Lorraine was in dire need. I could tell her spirits were lifted as a result of my agreement to help as well. After this visit, I was happy to do anything to help her feel better emotionally and possibly physically. I was shook by the visit but glad I was able to be a light for her, even if it was for a brief moment.

I set up the GoFundMe account for Aunt Lorraine and posted it by early November. It read:

Hello, I am Lorraine. In 2010, I beat cancer. I was in remission for 7 years when suddenly cancer returned in spring 2018. I was diagnosed with stage 4 cancer this past February. It has been overwhelming to say the least. My body has not permitted me to work in the last four months. Medical bills and living expenses are mounting simultaneously. I want to *Leave this Earth* with a piece of mind. No one should be left with the balances of my medical or living expenses. Therefore, I am asking for your assistance to get these expenses paid as I make my final transition. Thank you for your consideration. I am forever grateful.

It was the hardest post I ever had to write on multiple levels. It was shared on Facebook 213 times. And, we generated $2,450 toward her goal in very little time. It was not a lot of money, but it made my aunt happy and that was my only goal. She had some extra money in her account to live and pay some bills with dignity. I simply wanted to ease her mind so she would not be stressed, anxious, or distraught like she was the day I visited. She had been in agony and had not had any outlets. I turned over the security information to the GoFundMe account to Aunt Lorraine so she was in charge of receiving the money directly to her checking account. In her final two months, every little donation helped. She was forever grateful to the 23 people who donated to support her journey over the final days of her life. With each day, life was getting more intense and overwhelming as she made her journey to the end.

CHAPTER 18
RELATIONSHIPS

Labor Day weekend rolled around and I had been dating Tony Knowles since late June. During the four-day September weekend, he came to visit Arizona. I was excited to see him, but I felt different since Ravin Bridges had been coming around more frequently. Emotionally, I was torn between the two. Ravin had been my husband, and I reserved a sacred place in my heart that was open to his return. Seeing him more often only opened that space, and I felt like I wanted him to fill that void. But another part of me enjoyed Tony's attention, friendship, and understanding. Having Tony around for the weekend was fabulous. I enjoyed his company and conversation.

While in Arizona, we attended the ASU football game during the weekend. A friend, Becky Smythe, came along to keep Tony company during the game. I did not think he was a fan of football. My brother Gabriel joined us as usual and we were hyped about the game. Gabriel and I watched and analyzed the game as the season was early. We were trying to figure out the type of season the Sun Devils were going to have. Tony and Becky talked with each other. I had assumed they would have a lot of catching up to do because they had worked together for four years. With Becky teaching third grade, and Tony having taught fourth grade at the same school, they had so much in common. I wanted them to spend time with each other reminiscing. I know Becky felt as though she was an obstacle that night because Tony did not spend much time talking with me. I did not mind, however, and never saw it that way. I wanted them to talk and catch up us much as needed. I was going to get to spend time with Tony the whole weekend outside of the game.. Their time was limited; therefore, they should have spent as much time possible during the game to converse. Additionally, Gabriel and I were heavily invested in the game and really wanted nothing more.

The Devils won the football game and the weekend was off to a great start. We walked back to our vehicles and went our separate ways. Tony and I headed back to my house and looked forward to enjoying one another's company. It was nice to have him in Arizona again, but it felt different this time. I felt a bit of a wedge between the two of us, because, believe it or not, I was still not over Ravin. His presence was with me all the time, even though it had not even been a year since Ravin had left our home. I began to notice awkwardness between Tony and me.

On Sunday night, things got even more weird. Being as transparent as possible, I told Tony the story about coincidentally meeting up with Armando Wakefield at the WNBA Phoenix Mercury basketball game. I shared the conversation, word for word, with Tony even the parts about shaking his hand, asking him if he knew who I was, and telling him that we had so much to talk about.

Anthony's response shocked me. "Were you trying to intimidate him?"

Immediately, I shared that was not the point of my conversation with Armando. Instead, I needed Armando Wakefield to know I existed and that I was a real person. To break up a marriage without asking Ravin to work on it seemed heartless. Dating a married man and being one of the culprits in the breakup of the marriage was a horrible thing to do to someone. If they truly loved each other, Ravin and Armando just needed to wait until things were finalized before posting pictures on Facebook/Instagram celebrating their relationship and coexisting. That was a painful experience for me to watch, especially at a time when I was already under so much pressure with completing my action research. I simply had wanted to make a human connection with Armando Wakefield. For Tony to believe that I was trying to intimidate Armando made we realized that we were not on the same page.

During that same conversation, I shared that we were experiencing some challenges in our own relationship, particularly the distance, as he was living in Chicago and I was living in Phoenix. With the three-hour time difference, it was a challenge to get in touch with Tony. At times, I had to stop what I was doing in the afternoon to call Tony so we could get a chance to talk. Otherwise, if I waited until after 5:00 PM, I would miss the chance to connect because it would be too late to call. Also, Anthony did not live by himself so our phone calls had to be appropriate.

Being far apart from each other, we often resorted to talking on FaceTime. This gave us an opportunity to be intimate at times, but not when his parents were around. When his parents were home, which was most of the time, we could not explore any intimacy. Otherwise, FaceTime made it possible to see each other and masturbate to satisfy our human needs until the next time we saw each other in person. Unfortunately, the opportunity to have phone conversations like this was a challenge. I wanted more of Tony's attention and needed those intimate conversations more often for our relationship to survive. At this point, I was unsure how long our relationship was going to last.

About two weeks after Tony's trip to Arizona, he called me and asked if I were still feeling the same about our relationship. In particular, he wanted to know if I was still experiencing pressure from the distance. I told him I was still feeling the same way. The time difference was taking a toll on our ability to connect with each other. Tony asked if we could bring that conversation back up.

It was early morning, and I was on my way to work heading to the Southwest Valley. It probably was not the best time to talk about our relationship, especially if we were going to take a break. We should have determined a better time to talk instead of making hasty decisions as we were rushed for time before work. A little irritated that he brought up the conversation, and without much thought, I made a decision. I told Tony that I still was irritated by the distance. Our timing appeared to be off. I was having a challenging time connecting with him on a daily basis because of the distance apart and the time difference, and it also appeared my ex-husband was coming back in my life in some capacity.

In reality, I was confused emotionally in many areas of life. I should not have moved into the conversation, I did proceed. We finally decided while still on our way to work, even though it was not the best time for decision making, that we would stop seeing each other. We called things off and decided to try to work on our friendship. We felt that was best for the both of us.

Working on our friendship, Tony and I spoke to each other often, especially because we had worked together for four years. I saw him every day over that time and he was my confidante. Returning to the way things were before dating, I started texting Tony good morning messages. In one week, I believe I texted him "good morning" three days in a row. It was a Saturday morning when I sent the third text. To my surprise, Tony responded by asking me if I were feeling okay. I told him I was feeling fine as I was getting ready for a 12-mile jog. In response, he texted me that I was text messaging a lot. I told him I generally do that with people I care about.

In response he texted, "A text every now and then is appreciated."

I was shocked because we had been working on a friendship, and I thought this text was passive aggressive. I thought about his text for a few minutes. Finally, I concluded that I needed to take some immediate time away from Tony. His text message was hurtful. Tony always had appeared to be genuine so I could not understand how he could send such a text as a professional friend and confidante. I recognized that we had crossed over a line and became more than friends, but I never would have sent this type of text to him. I valued his friendship too much and I was afraid to lose him. Therefore, I quit texting him altogether. I simply pushed myself away. I thought his text was rude and mean. I just never wanted to do that to him.

About a month later, I got a text message from Tony. He informed me that his last text message had put a wedge between us. That was really intuitive, and it certainly had done just that. I did not know how to respond to his text message because I truly had been hurt by his original text message. After all, we had been better friends than we were lovers. And friends do not send each other hateful text messages. I did not respond to his text right away, but when I did respond, I assured him that perhaps we just needed time away from each other. I told him to reach out to me by phone when he was ready to talk about the situation. I felt comfortable leaving the ball in his court.

CHAPTER 19
NOT CANCER, AGAIN

I<small>T WAS MID-SEPTEMBER AND</small> I <small>GOT A PHONE CALL AT</small> night from my cousin Cherron. It was unusual for her to call me so late into the evening. When I saw her number on caller identification, I knew something was not quite right and I answered the phone at once. Cherron informed me the doctors detected that her dad had stage 4 cancer. Her father, my Uncle Ray and dad's brother, was the patriarch of our family. My heart dropped because I knew what that meant. I had been dealing with stage 4 cancer with Aunt Lorraine since February, and this was another death sentence. Although Aunt Lorraine was on my maternal side, cancer had now crossed over to the paternal side of the family.

I could not believe this was happening to two family members at the same time on opposite sides of the family. I felt like this was some kind of sick joke, and it could not be real. At that moment, I felt horrible for my cousins Joseph, Cherron, Dezi Rae, Jason, and Alisha.

And my Aunt Sandy must have had a hole in her heart. Once I was off the phone with Cherron, I felt devastated and helpless. I did what I always do in situations like this for it is the one thing I can control; I went for a jog. I ran for three miles at night around the neighborhood so I could think and put things into perspective. I truly was in disbelief.

While jogging, I decided I would be going to Globe the upcoming weekend because I was not going to miss another day without spending time with Uncle Ray. He had been the head of our family since Tata Justin, my grandfather, died in 2002. He was the strongest man I knew, and I wanted to do something to help. At the very least, I wanted to celebrate his life for as long as possible. Over the next two months, I went to Globe nearly every weekend to see Uncle Ray. Sometimes I spent the night, which always had been a rarity. Now, it was necessary. With each passing weekend, I could see Uncle Ray deteriorating right before my eyes. I knew he was not going to make it. He was getting thinner and weaker and even becoming delirious at times. This was the hardest thing to watch, but I turned to hope and prayer.

From the moment I received the news from my cousin, I knew I would be going to Globe to ensure that I spent as much time as possible with Uncle Ray. The first weekend I went to Globe, it was just like old times. I arrived and Uncle Ray was in good spirits. He was smiling from ear to ear because of being able to get so many family members together. The family enjoyed drinks and fellowship while playing corn hole in the backyard throughout the evening. It was a nice gathering of beautiful people. Uncle Ray and I unexpectedly happened to wear similar ASU Sun Devil T-shirts. So naturally, I took a picture with him while our pitchfork hand signal went up in the air. I felt a sense of urgency to get as many pictures as possible for life seemed to be so fragile. I was taking pictures of my aunts, uncles, cousins, and friends. It felt necessary to savor the life we shared. It also seemed like we all grew up so quickly. It could not have made Uncle Ray prouder to see us all together, and he gleamed. It was a special moment for him to see his family in one place although we had matured while leading separate lives. Just like old times, his family was near and celebrating.

I remember reminiscing about old times and looking at my uncle in disbelief knowing he would soon be gone. This man was the most durable member of our family, and it seemed impossible that he was going to die. The following weekend, I traveled to Globe again. In one short week, Uncle Ray already looked different physically. He was much thinner and had less energy. He was not drinking alcohol like the weekend before because he was on some stronger medications. Uncle Ray was strongly encouraged not to drink; as a result, he sat with a single beer tilting the can to wet his lips to appear like he was participating in the celebration throughout the night. We celebrated his wife's birthday with cake and ice cream. For the first time, my cousin Joseph spoke out. After singing happy birthday to Aunt Sandy, he shared that his dad would be undergoing treatment and needed all our prayers. The plan was to fight to the end. Cancer was not going to take my uncle.

It was the first time I had ever witnessed my cousin Joseph taking the initiative in this role. I could tell he was nervous and uncomfortable, but as the first-born child in that family, he really stepped up his game. I was impressed with his leadership. This proved that his children were going to do anything it took to keep my Uncle Ray alive.

Uncle Ray was weak and not moving much. He was sitting down more and complaining about how much pain he was feeling, especially in his lower back. On September 22, I decided to talk with Uncle Ray because I felt his days were limited.

Sitting next to him in lounge chairs in the backyard, I was able to whisper in his ear, "You lived a good life. If things ever get so bad, let it go and don't be afraid to walk through that door. Besides, Nana and Tata are waiting for you on the other side."

Nobody knew we had this discussion. It was our secret conversation, and he nodded his head in agreement. We always had a special connection, and I felt a sense of peace for being brave enough to speak those difficult words to him. To me, Uncle Ray was a father figure, and I needed him to know that I would support whatever he chose, whether it was to fight or submit to this terminal disease. No matter what, he was always a great fighter in this lifetime. I just could not believe cancer was teaming up to take two of my favorite family members.

CHAPTER 20
HOPE

O VER THE NEXT COUPLE OF MONTHS, I WAS DEALING with a lot of heavy emotions, but I held out hope. My Uncle Ray and Aunt Lorraine were getting increasingly sick; cancer was having its way with both of them. I was going to Globe every weekend to see my Uncle Ray, for I knew his days were limited. On my way home, I would stop to see Aunt Lorraine in Mesa who was now residing with her sister Debrah for her remaining days. It was a race to the finish line to see whose life was going to end first. It was a challenge to think about, but true. It looked like pancreatic cancer was going to eat away at my Uncle Ray first. Although Aunt Lorraine was in excruciating pain, her body was not deteriorating as quickly as Uncle Ray's.

In September, when I first found out Uncle Ray had stage 4 pancreatic cancer and started visiting Globe weekly, he was alive and happy to see family. He took on a positive attitude and had decided that he was going to fight. It was encouraging, and I had enormous hope. He was going to start chemotherapy and fight this deadly disease. I was inspired by his drive and determination. As I visited him weekly in Globe, however, he progressively looked worse. I noticed the pain in his face, and his body became frail. From one week to the next, his appearance took on a different form. I was gravely concerned, but I did not know what to do. I felt out of control. I could feel the troubling emotions in Uncle Ray's demeanor as well. As the cancer progressed, he lost that sense of fight. The pain was eating away at his back and legs, and soon it had a hold on his entire body. Our family gathered around him with support, but the hope was diminishing. It appeared like he was starting to embrace the idea of closing this chapter in life.

At the beginning of October, I had fall break. Before these two cancer diagnoses, I had decided I was going to Santa Marta, Colombia, for a vacation. The break had come so quickly as I had been busy visiting Uncle Ray in Globe and Aunt Lorraine in Mesa. I simply had lost track of time. With the trip to Colombia upon me, I almost canceled the vacation because of the condition of my aunt and uncle. I did not want to miss time with either of them. Quite frankly, I was afraid one of them was going to die before I returned from vacation. I spoke with my mom, and she assured me that I should go on the trip. Not to worry, she explained, if one of them passed away while I was gone, they would want me to be on vacation. Listening to my mom, I took the trip and text messaged all of my cousins on my decision to leave. They completely understood my position and wished me a great trip.

Santa Marta, Colombia, was a beautiful little town. It was restful and peaceful—exactly what I needed after spending so much time between my aunt and uncle as they battled sickness. It was a nice retreat from all the emotional torment. While I was in Santa Marta, I visited the construction site to a condominium tower where my friends David and Peter had purchased a home. We entered one of the spec apartments. They immediately started talking business as I was looking out the back-arcadia door. Suddenly, I heard the sales lady tell my friends that Phase I of the building was sold out, but one person was backing out of the deal. In addition, I heard her say that all the owner wanted was the $30,000 he had put down on the condominium in this building. Coincidentally, I had just sold a home in Phoenix and my profit of $30,000 was sitting in my bank account.

I joined the conversation and asked the sales lady if she could arrange a meeting with the current owner. I told her I was interested in buying the condominium, but it depended on how I felt about the current owner when meeting him. Quickly, the lady arranged that meeting and the ball started rolling. I was not sure whether I was really going to make a deal, but a meeting was set up for Thursday. I was going to meet a person by the name of Javier Cotes at a notary public office in Santa Marta, Magdalena.

We arrived before Javier Cotes. The sales representative, my friends, and I were waiting in the lobby of the building. Javier walked in, and I was surprised. A beautiful young man appeared. He was clean-cut and extremely nice. He wore a smile that stretched from ear to ear. Upon meeting him, I knew the deal was going to work out. We talked for a little bit, and I told him I was interested in purchasing his condominium. He was so grateful. The exchange of good energy must have been mutual because I felt a high level of trust. Javier was willing to sign over the contract and have it notarized. He also agreed that all I had to pay was $2,000 until I got back to the United States. Once I returned, I could pay him the balance of the money. I was surprised by this exchange. Javier must have felt strong energy too because he was willing to trust me in the deal for only $2,000. I only had known him for a few short moments, and Javier was comfortable with me returning to the United States before sending the remaining $28,000.

I could tell Javier was a good person, and I was not going to break the trust he already instilled in me. I no longer felt like I was making an impulsive decision, but instead, I was making an investment.

While we were at the office of the notary public, we transferred the contract over to my name. We had the documents notarized. I transferred $2,000 to his bank account, and I was on my way to eventually owning a vacation home in the Caribbean. It was an incredible adventure, and I was full of gratitude. I had no idea how all of this would pan out, but I was moving closer to a dream. The remainder of the trip to Santa Marta was phenomenal, and I had a renewed sense of hope!

CHAPTER 21
MORE LIES

IT WAS MID-NOVEMBER AND I RECEIVED ANOTHER PHONE call from Ravin. I recently had moved to Tempe because he was occasionally coming over to our former Phoenix residence. Moving to a nearby suburb put an end to those secret visits and permitted me to stabilize my mental and emotional health. Putting my phone down on the wash basin, I jumped in the shower to get ready for an early ASU football game. Suddenly, my phone started ringing. I peeked at my phone's caller ID from behind the shower curtain to see who was calling. When I saw it was Ravin, I simply shook my head. A part of me wanted to answer the phone because I sensed he was in need. But I chose not to answer the call and was okay with this decision.

Later, when I got Ravin's voice message he sounded anxious. In a raspy voice, he told me he wanted to donate to my school's annual turkey trot. This seemed like a fishy request. I felt as though that was not the real reason he was calling, as my intuition told me something completely different. Ravin never cared about my school functions or made any donations while we were together or married, for that matter. I was not sure why he suddenly wanted to donate something. Out of curiosity this time, I thought I should call him back, but I just could not do it. I was in a really good place and growing stronger each day in a new neighborhood. Any time I talked with Ravin, it took me a few steps backward. So, it was best for me to progress through the day without putting myself in another predicament.

Later, I heard from my brother Gabriel. As usual, we met up at the ASU football game. He told me that Ravin had an extraordinary Instagram post and asked me if I knew anything about him. I told my brother that I was completely unaware of anything about Ravin. To protect myself, I could not associate with him. Period.

Apparently, Ravin had posted an image of himself alone at the Gloria Estefan production of *Get on Your Feet* at Grady Gammage Auditorium. In the post, he alluded to having to go alone because his boyfriend had said he loved him yet stood him up for the event. Automatically, it took me back to his phone call earlier in the day. It all made sense now. Ravin only reached out to me when he was having problems in his relationship. Because he was feeling lost and alone, he was reaching out to me to make him feel better. I was glad I had not answered the phone earlier in that day. I have always known Ravin to act like a victim in these types of situations and attempt to draw sympathy on social media. This time, I could not be the one to lift him up while he was down.

For a moment, I felt sorry for him, although still I cared about myself more. Attempting to call him to ensure that he was okay would only be a roadblock to my development. I did not give it another thought while at the game. Instead, I turned my attention to Sun Devil football. I was happy to be alongside of my brother Gabriel in the grandstands at Frank Kush Field.

The next day was November 11. I planned a travel to Globe to see Uncle Ray. Before leaving, I called Teena Bridges, my former mother-in-law, just to make sure Ravin was healthy. My intuition was telling me that things were not quite right. I felt like calling his mother was safe for me emotionally, and she would give me some truthful insight. I asked about Ravin, and my intuition was right on target. She told me he was not well and actually felt suicidal. She asked me to step in and talk to him to see if I could get him to think straight. I did not think I could help because I knew Ravin and his narcissistic ways. But as I spoke with Teena, I assured her I would call Ravin to see what I could do to help.

My friend Tracy arrived to travel with me to Globe. We got in the car and as we approached the freeway, I told her that I needed her to listen to my phone call to Ravin. I was leveraging Tracy's company as balance. In case the phone call turned emotional, I would not allow myself to break down with Tracy in the car. Making a commitment is important to me. Because I told Susan

I would try to help, I needed to make that phone call to ensure that Ravin was okay.

As I keyed in his number, I was really nervous. Although I had made huge strides mentally and emotionally, I knew this could set me back in the progress I had achieved with getting over the divorce. I was more confident now, and I felt in control of my emotions. As I promised my former mother-in-law, I pushed through my feelings and made the call anyway.

To my surprise, Ravin quickly answered the phone. I told Ravin I had received his voice message and was calling to check on him. When he spoke, I could hear in his voice that things were unsettled. His voice quivered and was more raspy than usual. Sounding unusual, he assured me that nothing was wrong. He said he was fine and never mentioned anything about donating to the turkey trot as he had indicated in his message the day earlier. This confirmed my belief that something was wrong and that Ravin had used the donation as an excuse to make that phone call. I did not try to draw out any information from Ravin; instead, I told him that I had to trust what he was telling me.

At that moment, Ravin was not truthful again. I am glad Tracy was witness to this conversation because I had already told her why I needed to make this call before we headed to Globe. In addition, I had gathered plenty of information from his phone call, my brother telling me about his Instagram post, and his mother's disclosure about his suicidal thoughts. Instead of just being open, honest, and vulnerable to the man who loved him the most in this world, he flat out lied about his general welfare. At that moment, I decided I would not try to pry any information out of him.

So, I responded, "Okay, I am going to trust you are telling me the truth. I am leaving this conversation recognizing that you are well and doing okay." I told him I was on my way to Globe, and I would check on him later. I knew he was not telling the truth. I could hear it in his quivering voice. Ravin sounded scared, distant, and shaken to his core. Because I had been with him for eight years; I was able to tell when something was wrong. Tracy and I looked at each other astonished. We already knew the truth—that he was not sharing. He was not well or safe, and I could not do anything to save him anymore

.

CHAPTER 22
PRAY

AFTER RETURNING FROM SANTA MARTA, I RETURNED to caring for my aunt and uncle as much as possible. I wanted to devote as much time as possible to seeing them both. It appeared to be a race to see who was going to die first. This was sad, but true. Seeing Uncle Ray was heart wrenching. He appeared weaker and weaker every weekend I visited. He would lay down a lot and sometimes would not come out of his room.

One time when I was talking with him in the living room and looking at him while he was lying in the recliner, he asked, "Do you like teaching, *mijo*?"

This question puzzled me for a second because I had not taught in more than 18 years. He knew this before getting sick and had not asked me a question like that in quite some time. Immediately, I thought the strong medication must be tampering with his mind-set. I went along with his question and answered him.

Aunt Sandy chimed in and said, "Ray, you know he is not a teacher. He is a principal and has been a principal for a long time." Uncle Ray looked at me almost embarrassed. I wanted to reach out to let him know it was okay. I understood his misstep and the condition he was in entirely. Although I was empathetic, seeing this once strong man in this condition was heartbreaking.

On Sunday, November 11, a mass shooting occurred in my hometown of Globe, Arizona, which sent shockwaves across the country. I was awakened by a text from my childhood best friend, Melody. The text read, "Rich, there was a mass shooting in Globe last night. Cristi was one of the victims. Word on the street was that she did not make it." My heart hit the floor when I read that message. Cristi was Melody's girlfriend of 15 years. I could not believe this happened, and she was having to deal with this type of loss. I could not imagine losing a former partner of any type, especially one of 15 years. My emotions sank. All I could do was cry. I felt pain for the loss and sadness involving my hometown.

The next morning, I woke up and immediately called Melody. She was numb and saddened, but like usual, she was strong for the people who needed her most. She had practically raised Cristi's only daughter Breanna, and Melody was already planning on ways to support her, too. I checked on Melody frequently throughout the day. I hoped she felt my presence. I was with her through this ordeal. At one point, I got in my car and drove far away. I ended up in Tucson. After I recognized how far

I had gone, I stopped to eat breakfast and headed back to Phoenix afterward. I cried the whole trip and did not realize I had driven for such a long time. When I arrived in Tucson, I made a $100 donation to Cristi's funeral fund. It was such a disturbing event, a mass shooting in my small hometown of 6,000 people. How could that be? I just could not comprehend the idea.

I even received a text message from my ex-husband, Ravin Bridges, to make sure that I was not involved in the crossfire. He knew I had been in Globe that same day visiting Uncle Ray. I had just left the hysteria a few hours before.

Returning from Tucson, I went directly to see Aunt Lorraine. It was reported that she was not doing well and had a lot of pain in her stomach. I went to her side and held her hand. She told me that it was not going to be long before she passed on. Aunt Lorraine told me she was so sorry about my friend Cristi. Repeatedly, she asked me if I were going to be okay. I asked her not to worry about me. I was there to visit her, and I wanted her pain to subside. We held each other.

I was in shock, silently asking myself questions, "How could Cristi be gone? How did this mass shooting happen in Globe? Why are my aunt and uncle dying of cancer at the same time? How did I lose my husband?"

I had so many unanswered questions. I was scared inside, but strong on the outside. I did not want my aunt to see my concern. I was there to console her.

The following weekend, I went to Globe for a beer crawl with high school friends. This annual event had turned into a fundraiser for the victims of the mass shooting. The bars did not want us bar hopping or gathering in large numbers because they did not want to attract attention following the mass shooting. They usually liked the patronage of the alumni who occasionally visited the small town, but the shooting had the townspeople in fear.

Uncle Ray was also different that weekend. He was more withdrawn and did not come out of his room much. When he did come out, he lay on the recliner and stared at the ceiling. I could see it in his soul, he was leaving us, and the end was coming quickly. We had found out about his diagnosis only in late September and it was just the middle of November. Already, he was near the end of life. His backache had worsened, walking was a challenge, eating occurred only sporadically, and staring at the ceiling was the new norm.

A few days before Thanksgiving, Uncle Ray was admitted to the hospital. On the Tuesday before Thanksgiving, I drove to Globe to visit him at Cobre Valley Community Hospital. I felt an urgency to see him knowing that this might be the last time I saw him alive. I was hosting Thanksgiving at my house in Tempe for my immediate family, so I would not be able to see him over the holiday. In addition, the weekend following Thanksgiving was the ASU versus U of A annual rivalry football game. I would be traveling to Tucson to participate in the festivities and watch the annual rivalry game. Therefore, I knew if I wanted to see Uncle Ray, I had to make the trip to see him at once.

I arrived at the hospital with my mother. Uncle Ray was frail and laying in a hospital bed. His hair was gone now from chemotherapy treatments. As always, he had a smile on his face as we greeted him. I knew he was in pain because his voice was soft and almost inaudible. I was glad to have made the trip. As much as he could, he was in good spirits. He shared that he might get out of the hospital in time for Thanksgiving. I admired his hope and courage. Uncle Ray always put others before himself. I was glad to see his push to share Thanksgiving with his family in his home. He was truly heroic and inspirational to me.

We stayed with Uncle Ray for about 30 minutes and remained positive throughout the visit. As I hugged him goodbye that day, I thought it might be the last I saw him and so I squeezed him extra tight and kissed him on the forehead. Leaving the hospital, I looked at my mom and whispered, "He only has a week. I think this is the last time I am going to see him. I am glad we came."

She agreed. This man of great stature had deteriorated to a mere skeletal body frame in less than two months. I was concerned for my family. Could they handle this sudden loss? Hopefully, they were prepared and all I could do was pray. The next time I planned to visit was December 1.

CHAPTER 23
FATHER FIGURE
FAREWELL

ON THE LAST FRIDAY OF NOVEMBER, MY SCHOOL hosted a middle-school winter dance. It was my turn to chaperone on the administrative rotation. The assistant principal and dean of students had chaperoned the last two dances. I did not want anything happening outside of school to interfere with work. So I kept the engagement and chaperoned the dance.

The very next morning, I would head to Globe to see Uncle Ray for the final time, I was sure. I felt as though the good Lord was going to extend my uncle's life over the weekend, and I wanted to see him one last time. This particular night at the dance was extraordinary. Although the dance concluded at 8:00 PM, some parents did not arrive to pick up their children until 8:45 that evening. At times, I dealt with parents whose priorities were a little questionable. I was exhausted that day after putting in more than 14 hours at work. My goal was to finish the day, get some rest, and head to Globe first thing in the morning.

As I went home to rest, I just lay my head down at approximately 10:00 PM. Suddenly, the phone rang at about 10:30. It was my cousin Joseph, the eldest of Uncle Ray's children. I could hear the fear and desperation in his voice as he said, "Boo, my dad is doing really bad. I just wanted to share that with you." I promised him I would be up first thing in the morning, but if anything had changed to call me immediately. He agreed and we hung up.

At exactly 11:11 PM, I received another phone call from Joseph. He told me his dad had taken his last breath. I felt like an emergency alarm went off in my body as my adrenalin starting rushing. I popped up out of bed and told him I was on my way. The last thing I remember him saying was to drive safely. I scrambled to get dressed, found my keys, and dialed my brothers, Anthony and Gabriel. I let them know I was on my way to pick them up. I wanted to see my uncle one last time before the morgue picked up his corpse. It seemed as though the clock was ticking, and we were in a race against time. I had to get to Globe before my uncle would be carted away in a gurney. It seemed like it took me forever to get to my brothers, as I had to pick up one in Guadalupe and the other in Mesa.

After picking up my brothers, we raced to Globe. Once in the car, we drove in silence for an hour and 15 minutes. It was so quiet; I could hear the sound of my heartbeat thumping. I was overwhelmed with emotion.

It was late and the mood was quite grim. We made it just in time. As we were driving into the driveway, so was the mortuary's van. We parked in a dusty field, the first space we saw, and rushed inside. I had the chance to walk up to Uncle Ray and quiet tears rolled down my face as I kissed his forehead. I said goodbye with a little prayer.

I wondered, "God, what was our family going to do without our patriarch?"

Everyone appeared to be at a loss and no one said a word. We knew the days ahead were going to be a heavy lift. My brothers stayed back and watched, especially Anthony. He did not like to say goodbye, so he never stepped foot into the bedroom where Uncle Ray's body lay. I understood his distance and let him grieve his own way, although we were feeling the same great loss. It was colossal.

The mortuary personnel were cooperative and allowed the family to help get the corpse on to the gurney. It did not take long before Uncle Ray lay lifeless, completely covered by a white blanket, and then taken away to be prepared for his rosary and funeral. The next big hurdle was his funeral, which would be held the following week on December 8. The man was such a giant in our family; we turned our attention to celebrating his life.

As soon as the mortuary drove away with my Uncle Ray's body, we got into the car once again and drove back to Phoenix in silence. Before leaving, however, my cousin Joseph asked if I would give Uncle Ray's eulogy during the funeral services at Holy Angels Catholic Church. Without hesitation, I accepted. At the time, this appeared to be a huge commitment because my uncle held great family stature. Although I felt the pressure, I also felt honored to write a tribute to my father figure.

Once back on the road, we were tired but recognized it was an opportunity to have one last chance to say goodbye—that was much more important than any exhaustion. With this loss to our family, it was now time to prepare for the week ahead. Although we drove back in silence, already I was formulating ideas for his eulogy in my head. Once we returned to the Valley, I dropped off my brothers at their respective homes and went to my apartment to begin writing his eulogy. The minute I returned to my home in Tempe that Saturday morning, ideas began to transpire. It needed to be perfect, and I knew everyone was expecting an outstanding farewell.

CHAPTER 24
EULOGY

As the week progressed, my brothers and I were asked to be pallbearers at Uncle Ray's funeral. In addition to shopping for clothes to wear, I added to his eulogy each day before the memorial. I wrote, rewrote, and modified the draft numerous times. In addition, I called a few friends and practiced its delivery to ensure that it packed a punch. Uncle Ray was always there for me in this lifetime, and I worked diligently to be there for him, especially to support his family through this challenging time. Losing my uncle was a devastating life event, especially for his immediate family, including Aunt Sandy, Joseph, Cherron, Dezi Rae, Jason, and Alisha. When the time came and I stepped up to the lectern, I wanted to deliver a eulogy honoring a man who greatly affected our lives and empowered all of us.

Following is the eulogy I delivered at Holy Angels Catholic Church in Globe, Arizona, on Saturday, December 8, 2018, in memory of my uncle, Mr. Raymond Ramos:

Coming from a large family, I had 14 paternal and 10 maternal aunts and uncles. Needless to say, I got to build relationships with a lot of relatives over the years. As a child, I observed and listened to these adult figures in my life as they modeled character traits, some good and some not so good. I spent so much of my childhood analyzing these characteristics deciding which to adopt, who I wanted to be like, and what I wanted to be as I matured. For me, it was like shopping, making notes of the traits I wanted to collect and share with others while leaving those unworthy of sharing behind.

Through my childhood to my adult life, I am proud to say I gathered the most traits from Uncle Ray Ramos. He gave so much love and time, I am unsure I will be able to capture all of his contributions in such a short period. As I memorialize the life of my uncle, I am going to do my best to give you a snapshot of the man I consider a superhero and to me superheroes are legends. Therefore, Uncle Ray will always serve as the standard I look to pattern my life after as I carry on. It is with great honor I stand before you today to celebrate the life of Raymond Ramos. Over the course of 46 years, I observed a man who was strong, loyal, persistent, responsive, hardworking, and humorous. Simply saying these characteristics, I am already lifted inside with a feeling of hope. If I can epitomize half of these traits in this lifetime, I will have a positive impact on others. I say half because Uncle Ray set the standard high.

Joseph, this section reminded me of you.

Starting with strong, Uncle Ray had this incredible will to fight through life. He was protective of his family and did everything in his power to make sure they had everything they needed. As I recall, Uncle Ray exercised regularly. It was common to find him weightlifting or riding his bicycle. He believed in staying fit, building strength in order to nurture others. Right after Uncle Ray was diagnosed in late September, he told me he was still weightlifting to maintain strength. In addition, he walked up to six miles a day because he was determined to improve his condition. Again, I admired him because it was a true testament of his will to live. Recently, I was texting my cousin Michael Magana and we decided if there was one word we'd use to describe Uncle Ray, *strength* would definitely be the term, just like a superhero.

Alisha, I wrote this section for you.

Second, Uncle Ray was extremely loyal. He was there for his family and friends, his alma mater, and the Globe community. Everything he did was an effort to give back to his wife, kids, family, and friends. He sacrificed his time and energy so others could live comfortably. Uncle Ray also was a devout Globe Tiger. I think he bled orange and black more than I did. Recently in late October, I was sitting at the dining table in his new home and I asked him, "Uncle Ray, do you have my back?" He said, "Yes, because you have mine." In that same conversation, I was contemplating whether I was going to attend a Miami Junior High football game. In that conversation, Uncle Ray said, "I can't bring myself to wear green, Mijo, I am a Tiger man! I have grandkids that go to school in Miami, so I go to support them." I was convinced to attend that game, [where I] sat next to Uncle Ray and Aunt Sandy, and we cheered for Jaycob Goss. It was just like my uncle to do whatever it took to support his family, especially his grandkids, although his loyalty to the Globe Tigers and the Globe community ran deep and it's a character trait we can all learn from, a superpower no doubt.

Cherron, I thought of you when I wrote this section.

Third, Uncle Ray was persistent. If he wanted something, he worked for it and disregarded the cost or what it took to get the job done. Allow me to give you an example. When I was about 10 years old, Uncle Ray took me fishing at the Salt River Canyon. I packed a sandwich for the trip in a tin lunch box with an aluminum clamp at the top to keep it shut. When we unloaded the car, we grabbed our tackle boxes and fishing gear. We headed to set up on a cliff so we could fish from along the ledge. As I was walking toward the rock's edge, my lunchbox sprung open and out went my sandwich. As I was walking deliriously, I accidentally kicked my sandwich over the ledge and into the water. The sandwich was in a Ziplock bag so Uncle Ray decided he was going to dive in to save my lunch. From where we stood, as a 10-year-old child the cliff seemed steep to me. I was concerned about him jumping into the water. After all, it was just a sandwich, but he was so persistent to save it so he shed his clothing and jumped headfirst. He swam around, grabbed my sandwich, and climbed back to the top giving me the ziplock bag with my sandwich inside. Needless to say, Ziplock did not make their bags airtight back in the day my sandwich was drenched. I fed the fish with that sandwich instead of letting it dry and eating it myself. As a result of feeding the fish that afternoon, we did not catch anything. Moving forward, Uncle Ray was a superhero for saving the fishes' lunch. I do not think I ever told him I did not eat that sandwich. His persistence was a remarkable superpower act that made a lasting impact.

This section is for you, Dezi Rae.

Fourth, Uncle Ray was extremely responsive to the needs of others. He was aware of big events on all sides of the family. When there was a life-altering event or something he considered significant, he was there to support his family in one way or another. Uncle Ray attended numerous games, graduations, birthdays, retirement parties, weddings, and memorials. Not to mention, he had this unique way of bringing the whole family together. To him, it did not matter whether you were a Sanchez, Stidman, Miller, Calvillo, Ramos, Cummings, Magana, Casillas, or Madrid; you were family, especially if there was a drip of the same blood running through our veins. Uncle Ray supported all family regardless of what side you tried to stand on. He had this ability to bring family together and make us one group. He sacrificed so much of himself being responsive to the needs of others first. Imagine if we all adopted his superpower responsiveness, how much joy serving others might bring us.

Jason, I was thinking about you when I wrote this section.

Fifth, Uncle Ray was incredibly hard working. He had a work ethic that was unmatched by anyone. He spent nearly 40 years as a heavy equipment operator working in the copper mines near and around the Globe-Miami area. Over the years, his work attendance record was impeccable. He went to work rain or shine, regardless of his condition. On days he was not feeling well, he felt good enough to go to work. Uncle Ray knew that providing for his family was effort and meant working hard to ensure no one had to do without. He sacrificed time and was unselfish. As if working as a heavy operator in the copper mines for more than 40 hours a week was not enough, he cleaned yards for extra spending cash in his spare time. He hid his extra money in yearbooks, glove compartments, coat pockets, old shoes, and I am sure he had *petequia* like nana. This money was reserved for financial emergencies to prevent struggle. Uncle Ray's work ethic was impressive and if we applied this superpower, our careers would flourish.

Aunt Sandy, throughout this writing, you were on my mind.

Finally, Uncle Ray was also humorous. He laughed hysterically and loved to joke. Uncle Ray hosted barbecues and family events at his home. He enjoyed having his family and friends over and laughter generally took center stage. In his final days, he talked with Aunt Sandy about a burial site ensuring that she purchase a plot side-by-side. The reason they were to be buried side-by-side he said was so he could reach out and hold her hand. In another episode, while he was lying in bed, he reached out for his pillow and kissed it all over. When asked what he was doing, he humorously said he was pretending the pillow was his wife. Although Uncle Ray recognized his body was deteriorating, he never lost his sense of humor. I could tell you other humorous stories, but let's stay church appropriate. Uncle Ray's humor was another healthy superpower, and I look forward to continuing the laughter.

Like I said, I analyzed and observed many relatives since childhood. As I have matured, I analyzed character traits deciding which to adopt in an effort to succeed. Gladly, I worked diligently to be more like Uncle Ray. I have been watching and studying him for 46 years. I strove to acquire his strength, loyalty, persistence, responsiveness, hard work, and humor. I may not have mastered these character traits yet, but I definitely am proud of the work ethic he instilled in me. For me Uncle Ray was a living superhero; and if work ethic is the only superpower I develop, then education in my school building will always be exceptional for the children I serve. I am grateful for the standard he set. Uncle Ray set the bar incredibly high, and it makes me proud to try to replicate his example. To me, superheroes are legendary and Uncle Ray's legacy lives on in those he loved!

Joseph, Cherron, DeziRee, Jason, Alisha, and Aunt Sandy, I mentioned you before each paragraph above because you are strength, loyalty, persistence, responsiveness, hard work, and humor. Together, you will keep his super gifts living. My boy, Jayden, Uncle Ray was so proud of you. There is a good chance you do not know this, but since you started grade school, Uncle Ray always told me, "Jayden is so smart Little Richard, he is just like you." After getting to know you better in the last couple of months, Jayden, you are going to be better than me. And, I would be glad to help propel you forward. Addressing all of you, Uncle Ray may have left us in physical form but his spirit surrounds us infinitely; it's legendary. May God bless your soul Uncle Ray Ramos, I still have your back, and may the peace of the Lord be with you always.

As an educator, I deliver speeches all the time. Although I am used to public speaking, this was the hardest message I ever had to deliver. I was hoping my family felt I met the expectation by memorializing my uncle appropriately. He meant the world to all of us, therefore, honoring his life and memories accurately were necessary. I stepped down from the lectern, sought out each of his children and embraced them individually. It was as though no one else in the church mattered to me, just these six souls. When it came to embracing my Aunt Sandy, I hugged her so tightly, and the tears just rolled down my face. It was as if the floodgates finally opened, and I could no longer control the water pressure.

CHAPTER 25
FINAL DAYS

AFTER SAYING GOODBYE TO UNCLE RAY, MY ONLY FOCUS was Aunt Lorraine. I shifted all my energy and attention to celebrating the life she had left. On December 9, Aunt Lorraine had prepared one last meal for my Aunt Debrah's birthday. She was in agonizing pain with cancer now in her stomach, controlling her body, but she was on her feet in the kitchen making Mexican food. Aunt Lorraine wanted to prepare a meal as a gift to Aunt Debrah for always being there for her over the years.

When I arrived, Aunt Lorraine was exhausted. She was sweating profusely but finished the meal preparation. Obviously, Aunt Lorraine overextended herself and was not able to visit with family. She had to retreat back to her bedroom because she was in severe pain. She apologized to the family. Aunt Lorraine wanted to visit badly for she was always the energy of the party, but she could not bring herself to stand vertically. She reminded everybody we were going to celebrate one last time on December 30. Aunt Lorraine made this announcement known, for it would be her last party. Before making her exit, she gave me a hug with condolences for Uncle Ray's death as she was being escorted to her bedroom. I felt so empty not having my aunt at the center of this gathering. She always took the stage right alongside of me, but not this time. Aunt Lorraine had faded, and I never felt more alone in a room full of people.

The week before Christmas, I took the Friday off from work. I wanted to visit with Aunt Lorraine for as much of the day her body would permit. My mom and Uncle Gino were with her that morning when I called to make sure the visit was okay. They agreed, and they asked me to stop to get Aunt Lorraine some lunch. She was craving Kentucky Fried Chicken. Without question, I agreed to purchase a chicken pot pie with a biscuit and corn.

It was December 21 and, unbeknown to me, I was about to have my last coherent conversation with Aunt Lorraine. While we were sitting together having lunch, she was conversing with us as usual and making us laugh. She was sharing her opinion about different family members. She was so opinionated that day, and she allowed her thoughts to fly. It was a great reflection for us all to hear. Only four of us sat at the table, including my mom, Aunt Lorraine, Uncle Gino, and me. Aunt Lorraine was really content and appeared to be enjoying her food as well. To my surprise, she ate the whole pot pie. It was funny because she offered potatoes, green beans, and biscuits to others, but absolutely would not offer any of her chicken pot pie. It made me laugh inside.

Suddenly, Aunt Lorraine experienced sharp pain in her stomach. Tears started to roll down her face. She apologized and said she could not finish our conversation. It was time for her to retreat back to her bedroom. She was too weak to get up on her own. So, my mom and Uncle Gino lifted her off the chair and positioned themselves, one on each side, to escort her to the bedroom. Once in bed, my mom came out of the room and told me the time was near. A few minutes later, my Uncle Gino hollered for me to come back to Aunt Lorraine's bedroom. Because my hearing was bad, I wanted to be sure I heard my Uncle Gino correctly so he asked me to come back to the room a second time. I entered the room, and he shared Aunt Lorraine was asking to talk with me.

I lay halfway on the bed and grabbed my Aunt Lorraine's hand. As she looked me in the eye with tears flooding down her face, Aunt Lorraine said, "Honey, I am going to be leaving soon. I just want to make sure you are going to be okay."

I assured her that I would be fine because she taught me everything I needed to know.

She continued, "It is not going to be long, honey. For the longest time, it has been you and me. We have fought so long and hard together. We fought back against prejudice and we let no one talk about us in a derogatory way. Know that I love you with all my heart honey."

Although it was a struggle to hold myself together emotionally, I had to tell her to let go. She had been in pain for too long. I knew it was time for her to surrender this life and join the ranks of those who departed this Earth before her.

Aunt Lorraine said, "Be strong, honey. I will always be with you."

In response, I said, "I know you will. You and I have always had a strong relationship. Although it will be hard without you by my side, I will always remember your support and the love you gave. That will make it so much easier when you are resting. Thank you, Aunt Weez. I love you more."

It was time for me to leave. That conversation was important for the both of us, and I knew she would be resting eternally soon.

CHAPTER 26
HOSPICE

THE DAY BEFORE CHRISTMAS, AUNT LORRAINE MADE A brave decision: she was ready for hospice care. Aunt Lorraine finalized this decision when the hospice nurse dropped by my aunt's house to check on her. This was a decision she made on her own without sharing the information with anyone. When she surrendered to hospice, I knew her days were limited—less than a week. I was grateful to be on Christmas break so I could spend as much time at hospice as necessary. During my waking hours, I spent most of my vacation by her side as she was becoming less coherent.

When I walked into her room, she always lifted her arms up toward me and said, "Honey, get me out of here."

I would grab her arms and lift her up at the edge of her bed and hold her just so she could enjoy a different position for a few moments. This went on for a few days, until she was no longer coherent.

On December 28, I started the day at hospice. I arrived early at 6:00 AM to watch over Aunt Lorraine.

I knew the time was coming where she would close her eyes forever. I spent about four hours by her side before anyone else arrived that day. I had an 11:00 AM dental appointment in Avondale, so I needed someone to relieve me soon. This day was different. I could feel my aunt's energy strongly that day. It felt almost as if she were passing all her strength on to me. The experience was spiritual and uplifting.

When I first arrived in the early morning, she was startled by some noise right outside her window. The workers were moving racks outside her window, and she was startled by the clanging sound.

She jumped in bed and asked me, "What's that noise?"

I told her men were working outside her window, and not to worry. She was slipping in and out of coherency by this time.

At one point during my visit, her energy was so strong, I had this urge to write a message into the notepad.

I quickly wrote, "I am going to get back everything I lost in 2018."

I did not know what this meant, but I had lost a lot over the past year, including my marriage. The message was not clear, but I felt a powerful exchange of energy from Aunt Lorraine and suddenly had the urge to write this message. Time went by quickly, and my Aunt Roxane and mother arrived at 10:00 AM. I kissed them good morning and told them I had to go home, get ready, and head out to my dental appointment. On the way to the dental appointment, I text messaged Dr. Carlson, an ASU professor, to see if he wanted to meet me after my appointment for lunch. He agreed and told me to text him when I was leaving the dentist. I got my teeth cleaned and I was on my way back to Phoenix from Avondale at 12:30 PM.

I text messaged Dr. Carlson, and he wanted to meet me at FEZ in downtown Phoenix. I did not want to meet him at FEZ because it was close to Ravin's apartment. I knew he lived somewhere in that vicinity around 1st Avenue and Roosevelt. I tried to get my professor to meet me at a different location, but he was adamant about meeting at FEZ. I submitted to his preference and drove to downtown Phoenix.

As I was parking, nobody would ever believe my luck, I put my car in park and was about to get out. Suddenly, Ravin came out from this apartment complex straight ahead. I was shocked to unexpectedly be faced with coming in contact with Ravin. I did not know whether to run or hide. As I was getting out of the car, he saw me and headed in my direction at once.

He had a smile on his face and approached me asking, "What are you doing here?"

I replied, "I was afraid this was going to happen. I am meeting a friend for lunch and I specifically did not want to come to FEZ because I knew this was going to happen today."

Ravin replied, "It is strange because I should be at work right now. I just came home to get an Amazon package that was delivered to the wrong address again so I am coming to pick it up."

I told Ravin perhaps we should pay attention to this experience for the Universe might be telling us something. In all awkwardness, I asked Ravin, "So how is your relationship?"

He replied, "It is a mess."

I told him I was sorry to hear that because I hoped things were going well given that he had been so anxious to get out of our relationship and move into this one. Unfortunately, things were not going well. I told Ravin that perhaps we should meet up soon so we could finally talk. He agreed.

Ravin then told me he was sorry to hear about my Aunt Lorraine. I told him she was not going to be around too much longer, but she had asked if I had made things right with him. I asked him to be there once she passed away because I was unsure how I would handle life without her.

Ravin nodded his head and said, "I love you, Richard."

I assured him that I loved him, too. I told him I was going to head on to the restaurant where my friend was waiting. He agreed and we went our separate ways.

It was a bizarre experience running into Ravin because I felt that energy earlier in the morning. I was feeling powerful sitting next to my aunt before sunrise when I wrote the message, "I am going to get back everything I lost." I was feeling that energy and Ravin popped right back into my life. It seemed I was supposed to see him that day. I was not sure, however, he was the one I was supposed to get back, but I could not stop thinking about our meeting all day long. What a miraculous life event it was that my aunt was transferring her energy onto me.

On December 30, the hospice nurses shared the news that today was probably my aunt's last. Her body was shutting down rapidly with labored breathing. That afternoon, I got away for dinner with my friend Stacey just down the street from hospice care. In the middle of dinner, we were called back to the hospital because the time had arrived. We ran back to hospice, and I would not leave my Aunt Lorraine's side. I was going to be there when she transitioned because she was the female version of myself. Just two of us were left in the room: my eldest aunt and me.

At 8:11 PM, I watched Aunt Lorraine's body twitch once, and she looked at me with eyes wide open. Then she twitched a second time, opened her eyes wide, looked at her eldest sister, and took her last breath. She tilted her head to the side and her body lay lifeless. Aunt Lorraine was gone. Life suddenly was going to be different, but moving forward, I would be the light for the two of us.

CHAPTER 27
AUNT LORRAINE

AUNT LORRAINE'S FUNERAL WAS PLANNED FOR SATURDAY, January 12. It was a tough couple of weeks until her funeral. The family went absolutely insane. Her former lifelong partner Sandra was upset because she was not listed in the eulogy. People were squabbling over Aunt Lorraine's life insurance money, which was left to my Aunt Debrah, the beneficiary. We all seemed to forget the purpose behind her life celebration, that Aunt Lorraine was a beautiful person. We needed to keep that at the center. I felt like I was watching a circus and everybody was trying to be a ringleader.

For me, I found a sense of peace; she had left this Earth and she was no longer in pain. Feeling calm and at ease, I worked diligently to memorialize her in the obituary. I wanted people to recognize what a special individual Lorraine M. Ochoa was in this lifetime.

The following obituary was published in the *Arizona Republic, Silver Belt*, and *Copper Country News*:

Lorraine Marie Ochoa, 58, was called home to our Heavenly Father on Sunday, December 30, 2018, after a long, hard-fought battle with cancer. She passed away peacefully at The Health Care Center at Friendship Village in Tempe, Arizona with family by her side.

Lorraine was born in Globe, Arizona on August 25, 1960, to Irene Ochoa. She graduated from Globe High School in 1978. As a GHS student, she served as royalty on the homecoming court and cheered as the tiger mascot at Friday night football games. Also, Lorraine developed a love for music and dance while in high school. Along with her best friend Morris Guzman, she made heads turn on the dance floor as they made their way through disco and the 80s.

From Globe, Lorraine moved to Mesa, Arizona, in 1980. Quickly she adapted by making friends, networking professionally, and finding work in retail to save money to purchase her first home. Lorraine became a proud homeowner in the mid-80s and started remodeling as a hobby. It was common to find her painting, hanging ceiling fans, laying tile, or operating power tools to make home improvements. It was just the beginning as Lorraine sold, purchased, and renovated homes throughout Mesa, Gilbert, and Chandler. With every home she lived, Lorraine made upgrades and completed most work herself.

Lorraine loved sports. It was common to find her watching football on Sunday afternoons. She particularly enjoyed viewing her home-town sports teams compete. Lorraine was an avid fan of the Arizona Cardinals, Phoenix Suns, Arizona Diamondbacks, Phoenix Mercury, and Arizona State University Sun Devils. In her home office, she collected memorabilia representing each of these sports teams. Lorraine's loyalty for the home team was extraordinary.

As a consultant, Lorraine worked for Arizona Office Liquidators and Design. She attracted a large client base and designed innovative office spaces. Lorraine enjoyed her work and loved making her clients happy. She was trusted by her clientele and grew her base of support with her outstanding designs. It should be noted that Lorraine had an impressive work ethic.

Lorraine is survived by her sisters, Roxane Beydler (Terry), Margo Ramos, and Debrah Ochoa; brothers, Arthur, Gino (Christie), Adam, Joseph, and Nathaniel Ochoa (Tracy), and multiple nieces and nephews.

Lorraine was preceded in death by her mother, Irene Ochoa; brother, Albert Richard Ochoa; and nephew, Otto Downey. She also had a special relationship with a close family friend, Ray Ramos, who passed away of cancer on December 1, 2018. In the months before his passing, Lorraine empathized with Ray over telephone to ease anxiety over the transition between life and death.

Lorraine was loved dearly as a sister, aunt, cousin, and friend. Her pleasant smile and exuberant energy will be missed greatly. Lorraine will be remembered for entering a room and making lightbulbs in others go off with her ability to ignite passion for life. In addition, she had great humor, loyalty, enthusiasm, radiance, and unconditional love.

Services will be held January 12, 2019, at 1:00 PM at Holy Cross Catholic Church, 1244 S. Power Rd. in Mesa, Arizona. A reception will follow at Mesa Shadows Club House, 205 S. Higley Rd., also in Mesa.

Following is a picture of my aunt and myself. I am so proud of her.

The next hurdle was the actual funeral. Writing the obituary was one thing but writing her eulogy was another. The pressure was on, and I had two weeks to focus. I intended to light up the room just like Aunt Lorraine did when she would walk into a party!

Figure 2. Richard Ramos with Aunt Lorraine.

CHAPTER 28
BE THE LIGHT

After Aunt Lorraine's death, I simply allowed myself to rest. It had been two years of intensity, and I was exhausted. My body went through so much transformation in that period of time. I did not know what type of emotions would surface after all those ventures. The year 2018 was coming to a close and my good friend Tracy's birthday was on January 2. For two days, I shifted focus and set my attention on the new year and Stacey's birthday.

My mother, however, had other intentions. She came over to my apartment on New Year's Eve and asked me if I would go with her to Sandra Padilla's house to pick up the remaining items my Aunt Lorraine had left behind. Sandra was Aunt Lorraine's lifelong partner of 25 years. During the last days of my aunt's life, Sandra separated herself from Lorraine and encouraged her to live elsewhere. I was not quite sure what happened in their relationship, but I do know that Aunt Lorraine was hurt by the loss of her partner in addition to her declining health. It was sad to observe, but I never asked my aunt about the relationship while her health was deteriorating because I did not want to make matters worse.

When my mom asked me to go with her to Sandra Padilla's house, I gladly accepted because I wanted to find out what actually had happened between the two of them. I was not quite sure what my mother's intentions were, but I was looking for some answers.

When we arrived at Sandra's home, we were shown where the last of my Aunt Lorraine's items were, in a box near the exit door. Sandra asked us to come into her living space, so we sat down and started talking. It was a civil conversation. Although Sandra had her own way of dealing with the situation at hand, she appeared to be calm and accepting that my aunt was no longer around. We listened to her talk about my Aunt Lorraine's wishes to be cremated, planning a small Catholic church service, and coordinating a reception to follow. The conversation did not have much depth, and I decided not to pry for any more information than I needed. It simply did not matter what happened between Sandra and my Aunt, because it was not an issue after all.

Aunt Lorraine was not alive anymore, and she had been released of all hurt. All I could do was pray that Sandra did not have any guilt or regret, because that was not what my Aunt Lorraine would want to happen. She was a forgiving person so I hoped Sandra could forgive herself, too.

Over the next couple of days, I made *menudo* for New Year's Day. I invited my immediate family to come to the house to enjoy this traditional Mexican dish with me. It had been well over 10 years since the last time I had cooked *menudo*. Although it takes a while to prepare, it was a relaxing and therapeutic way for me to take my thoughts away from the events that had happened over the past two years. In addition to celebrating with family, I planned a surprise birthday party for my good friend Tracy. With her birthday the day after New Year's Day, I stayed with a Mexican theme. I made rice and green chile chicken casserole, and I prepared beans in the crockpot while I was at work. I made a cake and frosted it as well using a home decorating kit. Again, this was all a therapeutic experience, exactly what I needed to end the last two years' whirlwind.

I invited family over on January 2 to surprise Tracy, and we enjoyed another day of fellowship. Tracy was most definitely surprised, and it was a great way to shift focus to family and friendship.

After Tracy's birthday party, I began working to memorialize Aunt Lorraine's life by writing her eulogy. In early December, Aunt Lorraine asked me if I would deliver her eulogy by celebrating our time together. Although I agreed to do so, I felt great pressure because Aunt Lorraine's life was so colorful. I knew it was my responsibility to deliver a eulogy that would pack a punch. I had two weeks to pen memories that were all inclusive. At the end of her funeral services, I wanted people to remember her for a lifetime. From that day forward, I worked on her memorial every day adding and reworking each draft to make it near perfect. By January 12, I was ready to deliver.

The day of her funeral service, I stood at the podium of the Holy Cross Catholic Church and shared the life of Lorraine M. Ochoa. In her memory, it read:

> Aunt Lorraine and I had a special connection. Not only was I her nephew, but also I was her sidekick, especially in how others spoke of and to one another. She was strong, truthful, loved from the heart, and helped others. She was a trailblazer and laid the foundation for me and many more. Experience made her strong, resilient, and successful as truth was on her side. Today, I share the life of Lorraine Marie Ochoa as I experienced it from a nephew's perspective and partner in her adventurous journey.
>
> Have you ever idolized someone your whole life, so much you strive to emulate them? Aunt Lorraine was that person for me. Since the time I was old enough to comprehend the ongoing activities in my environment, I recognized the many gifts she brought to the table. Aunt Lorraine had this ability to light up the room with her smile and became the life of every party. Recently, I was having this

conversation with a friend, and he said, "What are you going to do when your Aunt Lorraine passes away?" Perplexed by this question, I said, "I am going to live on by celebrating her life." At which point, he said, "I don't think you recognize how this is going to impact you because you two are like the same person. You both are so loud." What a jerk? It took me a day to figure out what he was trying to say. Once I figured it out, I smiled because what he meant to say was Aunt Lorraine and I were outspoken, stood up for fairness, and always had a good time. She was tough, fun-loving, energetic, spiritual, and served as the life of the party. Today, I hope to take you on a trip down memory lane as I share highlights of Aunt Lorraine's life, the person I idolized.

She was tough. Aunt Lorraine hung with some of the toughest boys in the school yard and gave them a run for their money. As a matter of fact, she probably took their money. Aunt Lorraine could pass a football, tune-up a vehicle, hang a ceiling fan, operate power tools, and protect her loved ones better than anyone. She was athletic, not to mention an avid supporter to the Arizona Cardinals, Phoenix Suns, Arizona Diamondbacks, and Phoenix Mercury. It was common to find her covered in grease as she changed oil, fixed a flat, or switched out spark plugs. She enjoyed renovating every home she ever lived in by stripping floors, laying tile, and vibrantly painting rooms. Also, she had a knack for interior decorating and focused on arranging things her way; needless to say, she was a little stubborn. She took great pride in these activities.

Aunt Lorraine demonstrated strength by protecting her loved ones. She did anything to ensure her family and friends were safe, and sometimes that meant flexing her muscles. I always told people I never wanted to meet her in a dark alley when she was angry and there was only one other lady I felt that way about, Diana Taurasi. All that said, I truly admired Aunt Lorraine's strength.

Aunt Lorraine was fun-loving and carefree. When I was a child, she was my role model as she had the ability to make lots of friends. In high school, she was recognized for her winning personality as a representative of the GHS homecoming royal court, but denied the title of queen on a technicality in small-town politics. And one of my favorite memories was when she served as the Tiger mascot. I remember her in the tiger costume, standing in front of the mirror, painting her whiskers on her cheeks preparing for the big Friday night football game. I already was her fan, but when I experienced her energy in that tiger uniform, I began to visualize my future as a Globe Tiger. Aunt Lorraine captivated the crowd with her enthusiasm, which seemed to be the story of her life—*captivating*. If you were fortunate to be her friend, she considered you family with her overwhelming heart. Aunt Lorraine was fair, truthful, and outspoken; fighting for what was right. She attracted friends from all walks of life. When I attended Arizona State University in 1990, I lived with Aunt Lorraine. I have this fond memory of coming home from school one evening and hanging out in her front yard. Aunt Lorraine was a huge music lover so we listened to Black Box, and she wanted to learn the Electric Slide. So we cleared out the driveway and began dancing to Black Box's *Everybody*. As we began line dancing, one-by-one, kids from around the block became fascinated. Soon, we had all the neighborhood kids with us at 1334 West 6th Drive, rocking the Electric Slide. This is the type of fun-loving energy Aunt Lorraine exchanged with others, and this time it just so happened to be the youth in her neighborhood. She spent her life being and giving love.

I idolized her ability to be footloose and fancy free, all love.

Aunt Lorraine was energy. She was the kind [of person] who lit up the room when she walked in with a vibrant smile and exuberant spirit. She had this way of transcending her energy on to others, igniting a passion for life. The minute she walked through the doors, flashes and light bulbs would go off in the room, multiplying like a disco dance floor. Speaking of dance, Aunt Lorraine had rhythm and soul. She could ride the pony better than anyone I know (I think she learned that dance from Aunt Flo, but she enhanced it) and walk in place while grooving down low and working her way high again. I think she learned this from Grandma Irene because everybody knew she could get down; I called this dance the soul walk. Aunt Lorraine grooved to Michael Jackson's *Off the Wall* and rocked like a headbanger to Nazareth's *Hair of the Dog*. I remember when I lived with her, I was at home doing homework at the kitchen table, and Aunt Lorraine came home from a club. She put on Nazareth and rocked it out loud. Interpreting the music she did this dance giving the illusion that she was climbing the wall. Aunt Lorraine was a burst of energy. Whatever her involvement, she brought out the best in you whether you were family, friends, or a co-worker. Her personality was appealing, and everybody wanted to be around her radiant energy. I loved the way she multiplied enthusiasm; I strive to serve in that same capacity personally and professionally today.

She was a spiritual person. During our last full-length conversation on December 21 while eating at the dinner table, she made it very clear she was more spiritual than any of her other attributes. Aunt Lorraine explained she was spiritual because she believed in fairness, and sometimes books were biased. So, spirituality was a more fitting title. She practiced being one with her environment while acknowledging there was only one truth. Aunt Lorraine, as a loving being, was in charge of her own evolution and destiny. She did not believe in all that was written; instead she considered people to be complex who shaped their own outcomes through the power of the mind and spirit. It was important to her we recognize her spiritual beliefs as she confessed in front of my mother, Uncle Gino, and myself. Aunt Lorraine was a trailblazer; she was ahead of her time and used the challenges in her own experience to help others. I admired her spiritual belief because her love was all inclusive, and she wanted others to devote their lives to being the grandest version of themselves.

Finally, Aunt Lorraine was the life of all parties. She had the ability to draw people in and make them feel alive. Her smile was infectious. She danced feverishly and did not care who was watching, allowing her body to interpret the sound. Aunt Lorraine enjoyed cooking for others, too. A few weeks ago, she prepared an all-out, home-cooked meal for Aunt Debrah's birthday on December 9. In her own words she said, "Debrah does so much for me, and I want to give back by cooking her a special meal on her birthday."

If you knew Aunt Lorraine, she was a person of her word. She made enchiladas, rice, and beans on her own with absolutely no help. Weak and frail, she took great pride in cooking with sweat dripping down her face and legs trembling. She carried out her commitment even if she was near collapse. It was just like her to make people feel special as she sacrificed herself and worked tirelessly through pain. She worked to be the grandest version of herself, which was a true testament. For as long as I can remember, she was the life of the party, making everyone feel warm and welcome. When you made it inside her home, you were family, and found a place in her heart for a lifetime. I loved her charm, dance, smile, inspiration, and appeal to others. I look forward to replicating these characteristics in life.

In closing, Aunt Lorraine had an incredibly special request. She asked me to speak about her boss and supervisor, Robert Strauss. It was really important to her that I thank him for his exemplary leadership. When I asked her to describe him, she used words like *good, caring, loving,* and *generous.* Aunt Lorraine told me he not only treated her with the utmost respect at the workplace, but he also continued to support her mentally, emotionally, and financially even after she could no longer physically work. She recognized his support, and she was forever grateful to you, Robert Strauss.

Also, I commend Aunt Lorraine's three sisters. Roxane, Margo, and Debrah, what you did for her over the last three months of her life was truly remarkable. You showed love, empathy, and compassion for your sister with homecare around the clock. Your work does not go unnoticed and will forever be appreciated.

I stepped down from the lectern, faced the alter, and bowed my head. I walked away looking up to acknowledge my aunt who I believe will always be my guardian angel. I had delivered for her like she had always delivered for me. With a smile on my face, I knew she was smiling back. And this time, the torch was lit for two. She now lives within me and I will never let our light dim.

CHAPTER 29
ONWARD

HAVING IDOLIZED MY AUNT FOR MOST OF MY LIFE, I took her existence for granted. Although my Aunt Lorraine was no longer by my side, she left incredible memories for me to cherish for a lifetime. I will seek the opportunity to replicate her joy for living and making this world a better place. Most certainly, she made my world a better place. Now that she is resting, free of pain, I have found a sense of internal peace. When a person gives so much of themselves to make the lives of others better, you recognize the value of their earthly work. In that light, sharing her legacy brings me comfort and sooths my soul. I have turned the grief into serving others in an effort to empower them to improve in all facets.

Aunt Lorraine was the foundation of the Ochoa family. We all stand on the solid ground she put in place. For example, she loved the white elephant gift exchange she orchestrated year after year. At one point during the last few weeks of her life, she was organizing a white elephant gift exchange for family to be held on December 30. After recognizing how much her health was deteriorating, she unwillingly canceled the event. At the time, I did not understand the significance of December 30 or why she wanted to gather family and friends on this day. The date was after Christmas and before New Year's Day, so why December 30?

Perhaps it was her spiritual side disclosing that December 30 was significant because this was the day she was going home to Heaven. Sure enough, she gathered the family one last time in her life. Instead of a white elephant gift exchange, it was to say goodbye. That was the importance of December 30.

Moving forward, I will continue to focus on Aunt Lorraine, who was strong, fun-loving, energetic, spiritual, and the life of the party. She fought for fairness, equality, and determination. Aunt Lorraine always wanted to win. And ladies and gentlemen, she won. Cancer did not beat her; cancer freed her to be the next grandest version of herself. Lord knows, I will miss her greatly, but I am grateful she is no longer in pain and is now free to dance with all the other angels who went before her, including Grandma Irene, Aunt Flo, Uncle A.R., and Uncle Ray. I know she is listening to Black Box and teaching them to Electric Slide right now.

Getting a divorce, finishing my dissertation, losing Uncle Ray and Aunt Lorraine, and moving to Tempe were all life-altering events. It took a while for me to find my footing again. Through all of these trials, I did find some comfort and guidance. My Uncle Ray and Aunt Lorraine were such good people, and I vowed to live my life more like them. My Uncle Ray was stable, strong, and supportive. Therefore, I honor his life by supporting my friends and family and establishing the tradition that they have a place to gather on a regular basis. My Aunt Lorraine was energetic, positive, and the life of the party. With that in mind, I work diligently to help others see things positively and to remain enthusiastic on life's journey.

Their memory casts a shadow on the divorce I experienced. Losing my aunt and uncle made me recognize the importance of living life to the fullest. Although I miss Ravin desperately, I love myself more. I must move onward and embrace the new normal. We teach people how to treat us, and I cannot allow him back in my life after the mess he left. It was a cruel way to leave a marriage, but I wish him all the best this lifetime has to offer. He will have to carry on without me being a part of his life. I absolutely will not allow another human being to treat me or anyone else this way. Life without him is something I will get used to, I am positive.

CHAPTER 30
FINAL THOUGHTS

THE YEAR 2018 WAS NOTHING SHORT OF INCREDIBLE. I still believe in the philosophy that "my will for you is your will for you." But in a relationship, I believe foremost in trust and honesty. As a mature man, an open relationship had been the best agreement for Ravin and me. He was a younger professional, and I was busy getting my doctorate. If I had to do it all over again, I would proceed in the same way. We were together for eight years, including the time we were married. I was willing to make it through the challenges, including extramarital affairs. But we would never have made it if Ravin were no longer committed. The minute he said, "I want a divorce," I knew I had to let the marriage go—thus, my will for you is your will for you.

Although the nights were sleepless, I was able to maintain sanity. Early on in the separation, I recognized I had been through this experience before. Initially, I relied on a couple of friends for support, and they were there for me. Tracy met me at the gym early and tried to make me laugh as I was preparing to meet with Ravin to talk about the future of our marriage, and Tony listened to my rage after that conversation. Both were extremely supportive and friends started to surface like I had not noticed before. I needed them all the more when I realized how cold-hearted Ravin had become.

The moment he said, "Thanks for convoluting everything" at the beginning of our conversation about our marriage, I knew it was over. I began the grieving process and allowed myself to cry. As I watched Ravin's behavior over the previous years, I committed to leaving the relationship if he ever treated me the way he treated his family and friends. Indeed, he turned the tables on me, too, and I had to be without him.

Having gone through loss of long-term relationship before, I needed to make progress and move forward. Therefore, I put six interventions in place right off the bat. Those interventions included communicating with others, allowing myself to grieve, taking an antidepressant, exercising intensely, receiving help from a counselor, and ensuring I surrounded myself with good people. Communicating with my supervisor and the chair of my dissertation were critical to my success. Grieving allowed me to hurt and begin to heal. Although I am not a proponent of taking medication, it was absolutely necessary for me at the beginning of the separation. Exercise helped me align my mind, body, and spirit to stay sane. Visiting my psychotherapist was critical in knowing I could speak to a mental health professional for support. Finally, I was never by myself as my family and friends came to my aid. Each and every intervention was necessary for recovery, and I felt extremely supported.

Halting the writing on my dissertation and allowing myself to grieve was the greatest advice. I was provided the opportunity to be emotional to make necessary changes. Because I had been saving money for a remodel, I channeled the resources in a different way to upgrade my home. I hired help to paint the interior and exterior, rid my home of Ravin's belongings, and purchased new furniture. I moved fast and furiously because I only had a two-week window for the grieving process if I were going to complete my research in a timely fashion. Focusing on these changes at home felt good, and I no longer was reminded of Ravin's presence.

Staying the course with plans for Thanksgiving 2017 was pivotal. Maintaining a growth mind-set was a game changer. Having friends over and providing a feast were consistent with tradition and showed a great sense of integrity. When people had already committed to attending Thanksgiving dinner, canceling would have left people without a place to go for the holiday. Following through was the best idea and I was able to leverage the gathering as support in the healing process. Connecting with Crystal and sharing the story about Todd, the 13-year-old child, also were positives. I was reminded to find the positive in everything, so the loss of my spouse was not going to change my character.

Finding the good in everything is a good way to move forward. I was able to recognize that this separation was temporary and there would be an end to the pain. I was grateful for the Thanksgiving gathering and my family and friends coming to my rescue, giving me a foundation of support.

Receiving the text from Ravin informing me he filed for divorce after just one month of separation was a new low in our relationship. Life-altering decisions as such should always have been decided jointly for they affected us both. Ravin tried to be a martyr and shared that he would rather serve me divorce papers than have a stranger perform these responsibilities. Because I didn't have much choice, I took the advice to waste no time and sign the documents. Meeting him for the first time to sign, Ravin noticed my new hairstyle, body transformation, and renewed sense of confidence. This experience could have been challenging, but I found satisfaction instead. Getting these documents signed immediately helped to put these difficulties behind me. When I felt lonely, I became an intense writer in the company of others at various coffee shops as a support. In addition, I reserved time to write each day. It was the perfect storm of events, and I kept a laser focus.

After being served divorce papers, I forced myself to meet others, especially in social media circles. Although dating was much too early, I put myself in a position of meeting others to keep from being alone. I paid attention to the ways I was meeting people online and in-person.

I felt as though I was drawing people toward me with a new sense of confidence. The encounter of nearly being hit in the parking lot of Lux Coffee Shop led to a new friendship. It gave me hope for meeting people and coffee if nothing else. I forced myself to interact with others early on in the recovery journey. I learned so much about people and communication, recognizing that not everybody valued honesty.

I stayed the tradition course with Christmas 2017. Like the eight years prior, I hosted Christmas breakfast. Although Ravin was absent, I invited his mother, sister, nephew, and best friend. It was nice to have them alongside of my family and friends. At the onset of breakfast, I read a poem I wrote to demonstrate bravery and healing. It was imperative to let my guests know I was finding my way back and getting stronger. In addition, I showered each guest with ASU memorabilia. This was my way of showing gratitude to higher education for all of the opportunities I have been given over time. Once gifts were open, we took the traditional family photo in front of the house. The experience was amazing. Recognizing it could not last forever, I returned to writing the fourth chapter of my dissertation by that afternoon. But this time, I wrote with gratitude of having a successful life celebration.

My focus shifted on running a marathon during the 2018 Martin Luther King Jr. weekend. I had the emotional mind-set to run the distance, but I recognized I just may have been physically underprepared for my longest practice run had been only five miles. I persisted through the challenges, but by the end, my legs were in knots and cramping up. I also made strides in meeting new people even if my meet-up with Justin Ravin did not pan out.

I also was looking forward to meeting Andy Jordy and spending some time getting to know him. I kept myself busy between writing and going to ASU basketball games. The team was finding success under the coaching leadership of Bobby Hurley. Spending time with Andy was a great distraction although I wanted nothing more than a sleeping companion. I did not know how long this was going to last. In the end, being fair to him was more important than my personal needs.

My divorce was finalized around Valentine's Day 2018. Although this was supposed to be the close to a chapter in my life, I was on an emotional roller coaster. The new norm was to open my Instagram to find photos of Ravin and Armando as the newest couple posted on my feed. To me, this was not tactful, but it was not my journey. Mutual friends were checking on my well-being regularly. They were torn between sides, and I assured them they should not have to be put in that situation. When my divorce papers came in the mail, this was just another hurdle. I found solace in completing work and classes, exercising, taking antidepressants for sleep, visiting my counselor weekly, and finishing my dissertation.

March 2018 was loaded with events. During the month, I finished my dissertation and submitted the final draft to my committee. March 30 was the day set for my defense. I invited my mom, brothers, sister-in-law, and best friend

Pam. I practiced daily leading up to the event. In addition, I put together a PowerPoint presentation to use as a reference for the dissertation defense. Things were really starting to intensify. I experienced some lows during the month as well, especially as Aunt Lorraine was diagnosed with stage 4 ovarian cancer that had spread to other vital organs. I turned my energy to complete the defense in her honor. The day arrived, and I delivered a stellar performance. I presented my research, answered all questions thoroughly, and the committee made minimal recommendations for edits. For the first time, Dr. Kim introduced me as Dr. Ramos in a room filled with my committee, family, and best friend.

Graduating from ASU with a doctoral degree was a dream come true. I went into celebration mode and participated in all three graduations: general, teacher's college, and Latino convocation. I recognized the severity of Aunt Lorraine's cancer diagnosis when she did not show up to any of the graduation ceremonies. This never would have happened if she had been well. Receiving my doctorate was the ultimate celebration after a challenging five months. Graduation was a victory lap for rising up after adversity.

The trip to Germany was a gift to myself for finishing my doctorate. In addition, I had the opportunity to reconnect with my longtime friend Stephan. The highlight of the trip was visiting the German school leader and learning about their educational system. When I returned from Germany, I recognized life was different. I no longer was taking classes, nor was I obligated to write. I saw my Aunt Lorraine for the first time in months, and it was a fellowship that was long overdue. Also, I met with my former teacher Tony before he moved to Chicago. We both had a longtime crush on each other and crossed the line for the first time. Suddenly, my attention shifted to what was in Chicago.

Right before Fourth of July, I traveled to Chicago for the first time to celebrate Tony's birthday. Actually, we could not wait to see each other and made passionate love once in the hotel room. Because we were friends first, our relationship felt so comfortable. During my time in Chicago, Tony was an excellent tour guide. I could tell he was so happy to be back in his hometown. When I returned to Phoenix, I busied myself with preparation for my final year as a principal at Star West STEM Academy. Although I was occupied in planning, I really wanted to be in Tony's arms in Chicago.

The school year began in late July, and I had a new boss. On our very first interaction, she argued with me about our school's learning model and test scores. Anybody who knows me recognizes you should probably start by noticing the positive things happening at the school before criticizing. Needless to say, we did not start off on the right foot, and it set the tone for the remainder of the year. I was no longer taking medications nor visiting a counselor. I felt like life was getting easier, and I scheduled another flight to visit Tony in Chicago. I had one problem: Ravin came back into my life. He visited my house looking for his mail, and we planned to meet to talk for the first time since divorcing. I agreed to meet because I had so much to say about the end of our marriage. Initially meeting with Ravin, I recognized he needed the meeting more than I did because he looked distraught. He shared a story of his new boyfriend shoving him up against the wall, and I felt sorry for him. I recognized, however, that I no longer could save him. My emotions were mixed after seeing him, but I recognized it was best to move on.

As the summer was coming to a close, Ravin reached out again in late August. Knowing I am a season ticket holder to the Phoenix Mercury WNBA basketball games, Ravin asked if I would be at the game on August 31. When I confirmed I would be there, Ravin said he might also attend. At that point, I invited him to come and say goodbye to my family because he never did that before leaving the marriage. People in my family needed closure, and my niece Alynna was one of those people. Although I saw Ravin and Armando sitting below us in the arena, he never showed up to address my family. Even though he was a no show, I ran into his boyfriend Armando at halftime while I was going to the restroom. I stole the chance to walk up to him and introduce myself. In addition, I invited him to meet up in the future so we could talk. Armando never took me up on the offer, but the chance to meet him was no coincidence. Now, I was no longer just a personality; I was a real person and we made eye-to-eye contact.

After two months of not seeing my Aunt Lorraine, I forced my way in again. I was not spending enough time with her, especially knowing she would die soon. I made arrangements with her girlfriend to see her in mid-September. When I arrived, something was not quite right as she was basically living out of a guest bedroom in a home she practically renovated. Learning my Aunt Lorraine was depressed, I wanted to help. She asked me to start a GoFundMe account to cover her living and medical expenses because her work benefits were nearing the end. Although I was reluctant, I asked for money through GoFundMe on social media as a favor. As Aunt Lorraine was preparing to die, I wanted her to be at peace without the worry of financial obligations. If I could ease that anxiety by posting this request, I had to get past my misgivings and do so with humility.

Life changed again in the middle of September. As much as I liked Tony Knowles, I had to let that relationship go. Living 2,000 miles apart from each other with different time zones made it difficult to connect. In addition, Ravin Bridges was back in my life to some capacity and I wanted to explore why. It was too soon for us to be friends, and I was not over him yet. I asked Tony for some time to reconsider our relationship, and I maintained communication with him. When he snapped back in a text message that it was okay to communicate every now and then without explanation, I took offense. I had to end all communication with Tony because I considered him a good friend first, and I would not treat our friendship in the same manner. I recognized life was changing again, and I needed to figure out my next steps.

Soon after breaking things off with Tony, I found out Uncle Ray, my dad's brother, was diagnosed with pancreatic cancer. Uncle Ray was the strongest man I knew; and since my paternal grandfather passed away in 2002, he had held the Ramos family together. I had always heard pancreatic cancer was a death sentence, but if anyone could fight the disease, Uncle Ray was that person. Like usual, when I learned about his health, I changed my clothes to exercise gear and went for a jog so I could pray. While jogging, I vowed to team up with my family to support Uncle Ray for the fight of his life. I just could not believe cancer was eating away at two of my favorite family members simultaneously, Aunt Lorraine and Uncle Ray.

Every weekend, I went to Globe, Arizona, to visit my Uncle Ray. And, on the way back to Tempe, I would stop in Mesa to see my Aunt Lorraine. It was tough to watch them deteriorate. Unfortunately, I felt like I was watching a race to see who was going to die first. Uncle Ray's body was changing by the day as he was becoming frail. Still, I had hope that chemotherapy could save him. Aunt Lorraine, in contrast, was in excruciating pain and doctors could not do anything but try to make her comfortable. I tried to escape all of the illness by going to Santa Marta, Magdalena, in early October 2018 during fall break. I even bought a condo near the Caribbean on this trip. My spirits were lifted, indeed, but when I returned to Arizona, things were looking even more grim for my aunt and uncle.

As fall progressed, Ravin called me in early November. I was in the shower when I heard the phone ring. I peered out from the shower to check the caller ID. Once I saw it was Ravin, I decided not to answer, and it felt empowering. When I listened to his voice message later, Ravin asked how to make a turkey donation to my school's annual turkey trot. His voice appeared to quiver, and I picked up on other indications that he was not well. For one, he was calling me of all people. My brother had already informed me that his Instagram story indicated some trouble in his relationship, and his mother alluded to Ravin being suicidal.

Although I felt sorry for Ravin, I had to wait to return his call because I could not slip backward on the progress I was making after the divorce. When I called a day later, Ravin answered the phone but lied about his well-being. As directly as possible, I asked him if he needed help in any way; he assured me that everything was fine. Knowing Ravin for nearly a decade together, I could hear in his voice that he was distraught again. At that point, I recognized that if he could not be truthful, I could not help him. It was not my journey.

By mid-November, Uncle Ray was deteriorating at rapid speed. It was hard to witness his decline. I went to visit him with my cousin Shakira on November 11, but he spent most of the time sleeping. All was calm in Globe when we left to travel back to Tempe that night. I had just fallen asleep that evening when suddenly my phone began ringing with text notifications. On high alert, I thought something happened to either my aunt or uncle. It was my childhood best friend Melody text messaging me that a mass shooting had taken place in our hometown. She indicated her ex-girlfriend Cristi of 15 years was one of the fatalities. My hometown seemed like a safe haven, a place to go when one needed a piece of mind. Now, we had national attention as another massacre ripped through the heart of my hometown. It was devastating, yet the tri-cities of Globe-Miami-San Carlos unified to raise money to support the victims and their families.

Knowing Aunt Lorraine and Uncle Ray were on their way to resting eternally was paramount in my well-being for their health was rapidly declining.

Uncle Ray died on December 1. Although I did not make it to his home in time before he took his last breath, I saw him before the morgue removed his body. When I received that phone call, I traveled across town to pick up my brothers in Tempe and we made our way to Globe at the same time as the mortician arrived. I had time to pray next to his corpse and kissed him goodbye one last time. The man was such a family giant, it was hard to imagine life without him. The ride back to Tempe was silent that early morning, as we all reflected on the love he gave.

One of the most challenging things I had to do was deliver my uncle's eulogy. I modified the message to perfection over a week and practiced in front of others. I worked diligently to highlight his character and discovered his wife and kids displayed some of the same traits. Therefore, I referenced each of his family members and tied those attributes to each one of them. The message I was trying to convey was that Uncle Ray's memory lives on in each one of his family. I gave the delivery my all, and once I said the last word, I stepped down from the alter and hugged his wife and each of his kids. I had an incredible moment embracing each one, and every one of those hugs was different yet special.

After Uncle Ray's death, Aunt Lorraine became my sole focus. She was sad because Uncle Ray had died. Although she was extremely ill, Aunt Lorraine was still doing for others like cooking a birthday dinner for Aunt Debrah and planning a white elephant gift exchange for the last time on December 30. A few days before Christmas, I visited my aunt when she called me to her room. Aunt Lorraine looked into my eyes and told me the end was near. She asked if I was okay and reinforced how much she loved me. In my heart, I knew she was telling me goodbye. I reassured her that I would be fine because I had learned from her actions, and I would continue to be the light for both of us. I also knew we were no longer down to weeks until her death, but just days. I was glad she gave me the warning because it gave me time to prepare for the passing of the torch.

Aunt Lorraine surrendered to a hospice care facility her last few days of life. At that point, I would not leave the facilities. The one time I did leave, I went to a dental appointment and coincidently ran into Ravin in downtown Phoenix. Again, he looked thin, distraught, and reinforced to me his new relationship was a mess. Ravin appeared concerned that my Aunt Lorraine was down to her last few days.

I thought he was actually sincere when he said, "What are you going to do without her? Because you guys are like the same person."

I asked him to be there for me when she died, and he nodded his head. If he showed to her funeral, that would reveal whether or not he was genuine.

I was in the room when Aunt Lorraine took her last breath. She died on December 30, the same day she wanted to have the last white elephant gift exchange. Still, we gathered as a family, but it was to witness her transition instead. I believe that was the significance of that date and she knew it all along. With Aunt Lorraine's passing, I was overwhelmed with peace and serenity. It marked the end to an intense year that started with divorce. The year was fueled by completing research, defending my dissertation, graduating a Sun Devil, caring for Aunt Lorraine and Uncle Ray as they battled stage 4 cancer, and laying them both to rest. With 2018 coming to a close, I had high hopes for 2019. Although Aunt Lorraine's funeral was on the horizon, I could see the storm was calming.

After Aunt Lorraine died, I finally allowed myself to rest. At her request, I began writing her eulogy and prepared for another impactful delivery. Because Aunt Lorraine and I were similar people, I did not feel as much pressure writing her memorial. It came naturally as I included elements of her character like love, strength, energy, and positivity. Aunt Lorraine was also an incredible dancer, avid sports fan, jack of all trades, and inspiration to so many. Before she died, Aunt Lorraine asked me to ensure I thanked her boss Robert Strauss publicly for keeping her on payroll with health benefits even after she could no longer work because of her health condition. I delivered the eulogy and left the lectern. Instantaneously, I sensed my aunt smiling from above.

I am forever changed by the death of Uncle Ray and Aunt Lorraine. They were two family personalities that positively affected everyone around them. When they died, I decided to live more like them. Although 2018 was a tough year, I recognized many celebrations along the way. For one, I made it through one of the most challenging doctoral programs in the country while carrying a lot of baggage, no doubt. Two, my baby brother graduated from Grand Canyon University and joined the teacher ranks. Sadly, Ravin never showed to Aunt Lorraine's funeral, nor did he call to express his condolences. I no longer questioned his sincerity; his actions summed them up. My aunt had loved him; and when he did not show up for her funeral, I closed that chapter.

I am grateful for the resources that were available to me along the way, including exercise, counseling, medication, family and friends, and writing in public while surrounded by strangers. I pushed through the dark and found the light. To me, this was the best way to show I was not broken. I am ready for the next chapters in my life because I am resilient.